The Cricketing Greigs

The Cricketing Greigs

David Lemmon

BREEDON
BOOKS
SPORT

First published in Great Britain by
The Breedon Books Publishing Company Limited
44 Friar Gate, Derby DE1 1DA
1991

ISBN 0 907969 92 5

Printed and bound in Great Britain by Bath Press, Bath and London.
Jacket printed by The Nuffield Press, Cowley, Oxford.

Contents

In Memory
of
Sandy

THIS book would not have been possible without the co-operation of the Greig family, and I am most grateful to them for their help and kindness. I would also like to thank Ken McEwan, Mr Scrymegeouw Wedderburn, the Ministry of Defence, Surrey County Cricket Club, Brian Croudy and many others who have been such a help.

Introduction

IT IS thirteen years since Tony Greig appeared in first-class cricket in England, and the Packer Affair is now fourteen years in the past. It would be difficult for young people today to understand the impact that World Series Cricket had on the cricket world at large. It caused argument and broke friendships, but, directly and indirectly, it revolutionized the game. There was no sponsorship of Test cricket in England before the Packer Affair, nor was there an adequate standard of payment for players. Much that has become an integral part of the game was born in the Packer era. It was a revolution that was never totally understood by many who administered the game and, like all revolutions, it had its victims.

The main victim was Tony Greig, captain of England, who was Mr Kerry Packer's prime agent in bringing World Series Cricket into being. Whilst others who threw in their lot with the Packer organization — Alan Knott, Derek Underwood, Viv Richards, Clive Lloyd, Imran Khan — gained total rehabilitation once peace was declared, Tony Greig has, in some sense, continued to carry all the blame.

This book seeks neither to open old wounds, nor to excuse, nor even to blame. It attempts to put Tony Greig in historical context, not only within the game of cricket, but within the Greig family.

The book is concerned primarily with three members of that family, Tony, his father Sandy, to whose memory the book is dedicated, and his younger brother, Ian, the present captain of Surrey.

It tries to show the stature of Sandy Greig as a man and illustrate his influence upon all who knew him; and it attempts also to show the integrity with which Ian Greig has faced the cricket world in an attempt to be recognized in his own right. I hope that it is a book about people rather than about cricket, although the two must always be most firmly joined.

David Lemmon

Sandy

ON TUESDAY, 4 December 1990, Alan Jones, the former rugby coach and recipient of the Australian radio industry's most prestigious *Best Talk Personality of the Year* award, broke with custom when he gave an obituary at the start of his programme on Station 2UE in Sydney. Jones' programme is both serious and provocative, touching as it does upon a variety of topics, but the moving obituary which he gave was as unusual as it was unexpected. It was a tribute to a man whose wisdom, experience and understanding had shed a light on all who came into contact with him.

'A Scotsman died last Friday, on St Andrew's Day. He was only sixty-eight. He'll be buried today. He was no ordinary Scotsman. This man was, perhaps, the most Scottish you could ever get.

'He had a distinguished war record. He won the DFC and DSO, personally presented to him by King George VI. He flew fifty-four bombing missions into Germany during the war.

'He had a wife named Joyce, two sons and two daughters. One of the girls lives in Namibia; the other is in the United Kingdom. They won't be here today for their dad's funeral.

'This Scotsman was a man-of-letters. He worked in South Africa for a while. He was fastidious about the use of the English language.

'He was heavily involved in sport. He loved rugby and cricket. He coached both sports. He was an administrator of both in South Africa, and he was loved by blacks and whites alike because he was honest and straight. He was never intimidated by anybody. He used to live to the full the maxim of Polonious in his advice to Laertes, when Polonious said,

"To thine own self be true
And it must follow as the night the day
Thou canst not then be false to any man."

'As I said, he was a Scotsman. He lived in South Africa for many years, but was passionate about Australia because of his relationship with Australians during the war, but he was deep down, and always, a Scot. He loved his rugby, and ever since Scotland won the Grand Slam of rugby in the Five-Nations Championship a couple of years ago, this fellow used to wear his tartan trousers and his Scottish jumper almost every Saturday in memory of that great moment. He never went to a rugby international at Concord Oval here in Sydney, because he felt that it was demeaning that such a fixture be played at such a ground.

'He was ill recently when he went to England about this time last year to attend the fiftieth anniversary of the Battle of Britain. He didn't want to die in England. He wanted to come back to Australia.

'Two more things about this bloke. He was an alcoholic once, and he told everyone about it because he kicked the habit. And he used to go to AA meetings and he supported AA because he said you needed strength and discipline to beat alcoholism — and he had both.

'But I suppose his proudest moments were the fact that his two sons played Test cricket. Both for England. And one of his sons played twice for Cambridge at rugby and could have played international rugby for Scotland.

'His sporting moments would have been the proudest in his life because these moments involved his two sons.

'The grass is a little less green today. An innings is ended. Sandy Greig will be buried today. The father of the former England captain, Tony, and the former England player, Ian. There could be no prouder Australian, nor could there be a prouder Scotsman, and certainly no prouder father.

'He deserves to rest in peace.'

There is nothing unusual about a Scotsman dying in Australia or, indeed, in any other part of what used to be the British Empire. The Scots are, by nature, a race of adventurers, inventors and explorers, proud and intelligent; and Sandy Greig was no exception.

He was born at Bathgate which is approximately at the centre of the triangle formed by Falkirk, Edinburgh and Motherwell in West Lothian. He arrived on 5 March 1922, and was christened Alexander Broom. His middle name was his mother's maiden name. The noted geologist, Dr Robert Broom, was his uncle.

Sandy Greig was not from a wealthy family, but neither did he suffer from some of the privations that were to come the way of many of his generation in the Thirties. His father, William, was initially a radio and music dealer in Bathgate but the business was to expand into a department store. Sandy was to receive his preparatory school education at the Academy School, Bathgate, and his childhood was full of warmth and happiness. He was passionately devoted to his mother and, between them and his sister Isobel, five years his junior, and his father, there developed a close family bond which was to be duplicated between his own wife and children years later.

In 1930, when he was eight, his mother died, yet so deep was his love for her, so great was the impression that she had made upon him, that he was to talk about her and her goodness for the rest of his life. He was ever the man for whom consistency in love and friendship were important.

Sandy in his sailor suit, pictured with Isobel.

The role of the woman in the family was taken over by Sandy's paternal grandmother, and if a child can ever be compensated for the loss of his or her mother, Mrs Greig senior provided that compensation. "She was," as Isobel remembers, "a wonderful influence on our lives. She was a wonderful lady of the 'old school' — so calm and filled with faith and love."

Much of her serenity was to remain with Sandy in the years to come, however tempestuous some of them were to be.

On 22 September 1932, Sandy entered George Watson's Boys' College in Edinburgh, one of the most famous of Scotland's schools.

'The Hospital' had been founded in accordance with the will of George Watson, an Edinburgh banker who had died in 1723, to provide for ten resident Foundations. It had opened in Lauriston Place in 1741, and in 1870 the Merchant Company of Edinburgh, the governing body, were granted powers by Parliament to reform all the 'hospitals' under its management. Watson's was remodelled into a fee-paying day school and opened as George Watson's College for Boys on 26 September 1870. It had approximately one thousand pupils and moved into larger premises in Archibald Place. The Ladies' College was founded on a separate site at that time.

In 1929, the governors of George Watson's Boys' College acquired the former Merchiston Castle playing fields, and, in 1932, the year that Alexander Broom Greig arrived at the school, the College moved to its present premises in Colinton Road.

It is a school which prides itself on its family atmosphere, its broad-based education and its sporting traditions. They are characteristics of which Sandy must have approved. He left no indelible record of academic achievement at the school, but it provided him with a sound and wide knowledge, a sensitivity to people and to literature, and a reverence for the

12

value of words that were to be integral to his life and his thinking. Moreover, it is still listed in the College records that his main interests were in football, tennis and the Officer Training Corps.

Sport was always his passion, and whatever his involvement in, and concern for, rugby football, he never lost his passionate love of soccer, and of Glasgow Rangers in particular. In all probability, the war was to deny Sandy the chance to achieve what he might have accomplished in sport. This is not to say that he would have anticipated his sons in the international field, but certainly he was an all-round sportsman of no mean prowess. As it was, he was destined to spend most of his time as coach, organizer, administrator, commentator and spectator.

As we have said, he was a fanatic supporter of Rangers. He received pocket money of half-a-crown a week, which was a good sum in the Thirties, and whenever Rangers were at home on a Saturday he would take the train from Bathgate to Waverley Station, Edinburgh. From Edinburgh, he would journey to Glasgow by train and then take a tram to the match at Ibrox Park. After watching the game, and these were vintage days for the Rangers, he would buy fish and chips, ten Woodbines and make the return journey involving tram and train. There would still be something left out of his half-a-crown for the rest of the week.

This passion for Rangers never deserted him and if there were depressions in later life, they were triggered by one of two things, no news of success by Tony in England and defeat for Rangers in Scotland. Such miserable days would mean an extra bottle.

"We used to lie on the floor in our home in Queenstown," says Ian, "and listen to this crackly voice give the county scores. Our most miserable days were when Tony didn't get runs, or when we didn't hear his name mentioned on the World Service of the BBC.

If he didn't hear Tony's name, and he might have taken 3 for 30, but that wasn't mentioned because John Snow had taken 5 for 60, Dad got into a terrible state of depression because Tony hadn't done well. The other problem was if Rangers lost. We always had a miserable Sunday if we heard that on the football scores."

Sandy Greig left George Watson's Boys' College at the end of the summer term, 26 July 1938. He joined the Mercantile Bank of India and left Scotland to travel to London to take up work as a bank clerk in Gracechurch Street in the City.

These were troublesome times. German troops marched into Austria. Neville Chamberlain returned from Munich and waved his piece of paper. It was the time of:

Hodza, Henlein, Hitler, The Maginot Line, The
heavy panic that cramps the lungs and presses The
collar down the spine.

People moved in a sense of bewilderment and unreality, seeking escape in pleasure. They thought, as Louis MacNeice wrote, that:

'This must be wrong, it has happened before,
Just like this before, we must be dreaming;
It was long ago these flies
Buzzed like this, so why are they still bombarding
The ears if not the eyes?'

Soon, the eyes too were to be bombarded as Europe, festered by Fascism, moved inexorably towards war.

On Sunday, 3 September 1939, Chamberlain announced that a state of war now existed between Great Britain and Germany. The following day, Monday the fourth, Alexander Broom Greig was among the first volunteers to arrive at the Royal Air Force Number One Unit Depot at Uxbridge. In enlisting as soon as the war broke out, he was doing exactly as his father had done in August 1914.

There was a barrier to be overcome before Sandy Greig could join the Royal Air Force. He was still six months short of his eighteenth birthday. In order to surmount the problem, he took the simple step of stating that he had been born in 1921, and not 1922, and that he had been at George Watson's College from *1931* until 1938. His father supported him by verifying what was, in fact, a falsification, for he knew that his son was determined to fly and that his enlistment was the logical conclusion of the interests that he had followed at school.

Sandy stood just over six feet tall, had blue eyes, fair hair and carried a small scar over his left eye, the legacy of a sporting injury. He was now 900821 A/ C 2 Greig, and, as such, he appeared before an Air Crew Selection Board on Tuesday, 5 September 1939. Physically and mentally, he was everything that the Board was looking for, and he was recommended for training as a pilot and for a commission.

Throughout his initial training in England and, from April 1940, in Southern Rhodesia, now Zimbabwe, Sandy Greig won high commendation for attitude, aptitude and fitness. Nevertheless, it was decided that his future was as an observer rather than as a pilot. By the beginning of 1941, he was qualified as a navigator although he was still some months away from operational flying.

It is necessary to pause and reflect for a moment on the part that Bomber Command, and the navigators in that command, were to play in bringing about a successful conclusion to the war.

Throughout the Thirties, a vigorous debate had been conducted in political and military circles about the practicality of strategic bombing, the long-range attacks on the centres of the enemy's war machine. There were great fears as to the number of innocent civilians that would be killed if such a campaign were conducted; and there was concern as to what public reaction would be in these circumstances. These fears contributed much to the policy of appeasement that allowed Hitler his bloodless conquests between 1936 and 1939.

By the outbreak of war, it was realized that the Germans had a massive advantage in air power, and one that could prove decisive, but, for all the misery inflicted by the Blitz on London and by raids on other towns and cities in Great Britain, the Germans never developed an effective strategic bombing policy. The Blitz was a failure, serving mainly to strengthen British resolve, and the critical targets in the Soviet Union were out of reach. Ultimately, it was the British Bomber Command, and the United States Army Air Force, which were to tilt the balance of the war.

In September 1939, RAF Bomber Command consisted of 272 twin-engined aircraft grouped in 17 squadrons. For the first eight months of the war, they conducted daylight raids on military targets and suffered heavy losses whilst inflicting little damage. At night, Whitley bombers were dropping propaganda leaflets on densely populated areas.

The dropping of leaflets was greeted with contempt, but it was an exercise that was not without benefits, for the British aircraft were groping around in the dark without radio navigation and with little idea where they were. The leaflet raids were discontinued when the Germans had taken control of the European mainland and bombing raids were the only means available to Britain to hit back at the enemy.

From the point of view of morale and sustaining the war effort, such raids were essential, but, in practice, they were worse than disappointing. The attempts to eliminate the German Navy's warships at Brest and ports and harbours in Northern Germany and to destroy the transport system in the Ruhr were unsuccessful. The reason was not hard to find. A serious scientific study, made in August 1941, revealed that only one bomber in ten was dropping its bombs even as close as five miles to its target. Navigation was the key problem.

The appointment of Air Marshal Arthur Harris as Commander-in-Chief Royal Air Force Bomber Command on 22 February 1942, was to have a positive influence on the course of the war. Harris was professional in approach and determined in attitude. His impact was immediate, and he was aided by technological advances such as the arrival of new aircraft, the Stirling, the Halifax and the Lancaster, and by the advent of the radion navigational aid known as Gee.

Sandy Greig, his training complete, was granted a commission for the duration of hostilities with effect from 17 May 1941. As Pilot Officer A.B.Greig, he joined 218 Squadron at Marham in Norfolk two months later and was entrusted with general air-crew duties. By the end of the year, he was operating as an observer on Wellingtons and Stirlings, and by the middle of 1942, having been promoted to the rank of Flying Officer, he was used as a navigator, the skill in which he had been specially trained.

These were strained, difficult and relentless times which demanded the commitment and courage of many, but Sandy Greig's qualities as an airman and as a man were recognized as exceptional. Towards the end of 1941 he received lacerations of the face and a broken nose when his aircraft was damaged. Part of the face below the lower lip was to be left without feeling for the rest of his life. In September 1942, he was awarded the Distinguished Flying Cross. Whilst returning from a bombing raid, his aircraft was under heavy flak, but with total disregard for his own safety, he attended to wounded colleagues. "I well remember," says his sister Isobel, "the thrill of going to Buckingham Palace with Dad to see him receive his medal from King George VI."

This was not the only way in which Sandy Greig's

prowess was recognized. At the end of August 1942, he was appointed acting Flight Lieutenant (paid) and a month later was posted to 101 Squadron as Squadron Navigation Officer.

The 101 Squadron had just been transferred to 1 Group and moved to Holme-on-Spalding Moor, north of the Humber between Selby and Hull, in order to rearm with the Avro Lancaster. Holme was a purpose-built Bomber Command station, and 101 Squadron was one of the first three squadrons to re-equip with the Lancaster, the first two of which arrived at the station on 11 October 1942. The problem was that air crews needed conversion training to cope with the new planes, but there was now a far greater sense of organization and specialization within Bomber Command. It was this more intelligent and purposeful planning that brought Greig, a man of proven ability, to 101 Squadron as Navigation Officer on 1 October, 1942.

An enthusiast who was both popular and respected, Sandy Greig struck up a particular friendship with Tony Reddick, who had been in the RAF since the Twenties and who had risen through the ranks. Reddick was recognized as a pilot of outstanding ability, and, as W.A.Scrymgeouw-Wedderburn, a colleague and friend, remembers, Reddick and Greig became 'partners in crime' and, given the opportunity, they always flew on operations together.

When Tony Reddick became squadron commander in January 1943, they thought that it would be better if they appeared less in each other's company, but they remained firm friends. Tony Reddick settled in Australia after he left the RAF, and he and Sandy met there when Tony Greig was playing in a Test match.

Sandy Greig was excited about the improvements that were taking place within Bomber Command.

'With Harris and Reddick in command, we started doing things we had not done before. In the old days we flew a mission and the air test beforehand, and that was that. Now we did formation and flying practice and bombing and gunnery exercises over the UK. Our ground training programme also increased considerably, as Squadron Navigation Officer I tried to improve the standard of navigation by discussing errors made with the crews. By doing other things like dinghy drills, the whole crew discipline on the squadron improved. It was noticeable that those crews whose discipline on the ground and in the air was good were the ones most inclined to survive. In fact I would go so far as to say that for those of us who had done a bit of operational flying, it wasn't difficult to pick out the crews who wouldn't survive. Of course, good crews didn't come back if luck was against them, but the most efficient crews were usually the lucky ones, and we used to say that the more crews practiced, the luckier they got.'

It is worth remembering that in the two years between September 1942, and September 1944, Bomber Command lost 30,500 air crew killed in action.

Sandy Greig's contribution to the increase of efficiency of the squadron, his analytical ability and his vision, were quickly recognized. At the beginning of 1943, there were two flight commanders under Tony Reddick, each of whom was responsible for ten aircraft and their crews. The squadron complement, however, had grown to thirty aircraft which meant that it was necessary to create a third flight.

It was customary to fill the posts of Squadron Commander and Flight Commander with pilots, but Observer Officers of outstanding ability could be recommended to the Commander-in-Chief. On 25 March 1943, such a recommendation was made.

'Flying Officer (Acting Flight Lieutenant)
A.B.Greig DFC — 68753
Navigator — No 101 Squadron — Holme
1. Under the provisions of your letter BC/C. 23068/P

dated 20 October 1942, authority is requested for the above-named Navigation Officer to be reposted to No 101 Squadron to fill the post of a Flight Commander consequent on the formation of a third Flight.

2. This officer has completed one operational tour and six sorties of his present tour. He is an exceptionally able officer and moreover, has an outstanding enthusiasm for flying, particularly operational flying, in which he has shown great ability not only as a navigator but also as an officer. He possesses pronounced organizing abilities and has powers of leadership and personality which mark him as fully qualified for the post of Flight Commander.

3. I strongly recommend this appointment as a special case.

E.A.B.Rice
Air Vice-Marshal
AOC 1 Group.'

Air Vice-Marshal Rice's recommendation was approved on 2 April, and, less than a month after his twenty-first birthday, Sandy Greig was acting Squadron Leader in command of C Flight of 101 Squardron. So highly was he valued that he was offered a permanent commission within weeks of this appointment, but he refused.

Greig's appointment as Flight Commander coincided with 101 Squadron being moved from Hulme to Ludford Magna. Situated between Louth and Market Rasen, Ludford airfield was built by the firm of George Wimpey in ninety days, but it was hardly the most comfortable of stations.

Scrymegeouw-Wedderburn recalls: "Sandy left Holme-on-Spalding Moor sometime in May 1943, and went to Ludford Magna where he was in charge of the preparations of the new station, ready for the arrival of the squadron which took place on 15 June.

"I myself had had leave and collected my car, which

Squadron-leader A.B.'Sandy' Greig, DSO, DFC.

I left at Ludford before going back to Holme — so overland transport was laid on.

"To digress for a moment. When I had finished my tour I was approached by members of the RAF Central Medical Establishment, who wanted to find out the make up of a successful operational pilot. When asked what I did in my spare time I replied that I went out and drank beer and occasionally went out with a girl.

'You must do something else,' they said.

'I don't,' I said.

"We were doing two nights on and one night off at this period.

"The same thing applied to Sandy, so, on the evening of 15 June, having flown in from Holme that day, it was into the car and off to the Royal Oak in Little Cawthorpe, some five or six miles away. The Lills who owned it became very good friends, and we got to know most of the people round about."

The RAF took no conscripted men for its air crew during the war, but relied entirely on volunteers, of whom there were plenty. A large proportion of these volunteers came from all parts of the globe and, by June 1943, more than a third of the pilots in Bomber Command were Australians, Canadians or New Zealanders.

Sandy Greig's C Flight had a preponderence of Australians, and it was his dealings with these men that gave him his admiration for them and for their country, although these dealings were not without their problems.

'My Australians were absolutely magnificent in the air, but on the ground they were just about uncontrollable. They were a law unto themselves, they overstayed their leave, they did as they pleased, and a severe reprimand meant nothing to them while the loss of a day's pay was like water off a duck's back. The Aussies were the most courageous bunch on the squadron, and I was very happy to see them on board

22

an aeroplane, but on the ground they put years on my life.'

Air Vice-Marshal Rice had emphasized Sandy's qualities as an officer when he recommended him for the post of Flight Commander. In particular, he had mentioned his powers of leadership and his strength of personality, characteristics which were to emerge in his sons. The powers of leadership were founded upon his understanding of, and concern for, those in his charge. Greig was fully appreciative of the unity necessary in a successful squadron and was quick to give praise to the ground crews in their multitude of trades whose expertise made operations possible. 'As far as I am concerned, the non-flying personnel of 101 were quite outstanding,' he said, 'and that applied to everyone on the station.'

Operations ranged far afield, with strategic targets in the industrial areas of Northern Italy being high on the list of Bomber Command priorities and on the list of missions entrusted to 101 Squadron. These operations were hazardous and took their toll of the squadron. One of the most depressing but necessary tasks that would fall to an officer of Sandy Greig's position was when, in the company of two NCOs from ground crew, he would have to collect all the personal effects in the morning from the bunks of those who had not returned from the raid the night before. To gather up the photographs of wife, children and parents and letters of love that had not been posted, as well as mascots and mementos, for dispatch to next of kin was a task that none enjoyed. One was dealing with the personal belongings and intimacies of men who had been one's friends and companions in arms. Mackay of 101 Squadron confessed that when he had the job: 'At the end of it all I went to the Mess and stood there until friends dragged me off to bed paralysed with drink.'

Alcohol was both a source of social enjoyment and

of refuge for young men in their early twenties who were being asked to bear burdens beyond their years.

Sandy Greig was only the second navigator in Bomber Command to be honoured with a Flight Commander's post, and a greater honour followed soon after when, on 23 August 1943, there was the immediate award of the Distinguished Service Order, a rare occurence. The citation in the *London Gazette* read as follows.

This officer, who has completed many sorties since being awarded the Distinguished Flying Cross, is a fearless and courageous captain. His great navigational ability and fine fighting qualities have inspired all with whom he has flown and have played a large part in the many successes obtained. His record of achievement is worthy of the highest praise.

Within days of this citation appearing, Sandy Greig received a telegram of 'warmest congratulation' from 'Bomber' Harris, the Commander-in-Chief Bomber Command. No praise could come higher than this, and it confirmed the esteem in which Greig was held. He was, it must be remembered, still six months short of his twenty-second birthday.

His reaction to the award was as one might have expected. 'I did not regard it as an award to me personally, rather I saw it as an award to my crew as an appreciation of the work of the Squadron.'

Scrymegeouw-Wedderburn recalled an amusing incident connected with the award of Sandy's DSO.

"On the evening of the day that Sandy's immediate DSO came through, he asked me to stop in Louth while he got his friend Sally to stitch on his DSO ribbon. However, he returned with haste to the car. Apparently Sally was getting married the next day! So Mrs Lill at the Royal Oak did it for him."

Sandy and Scrym Wedderburn were close friends. They discovered that they had common ground from before the war in the Crammond Inn outside Edinburgh. It was a favourite haunt of the Greigs, and Sandy's father would lunch there once a week after a round of golf in the years immediately after the war.

When Sandy and Scrym Wedderburn had been on operations on the same night, they would stay up to compare their bombing photographs and the respective successes of their mission once they had been developed.

Greig was a man of tremendous zest and enthusiasm, and these qualities were allied to a sense of energetic professionalism in his work. 'He was a real live wire,' writes Scrym Wedderburn, 'and, in fact, the only flying friend of mine to survive the war.'

The work of all concerned in Bomber Command was taxing both physically and mentally. The squadron crews were given preliminary warning that they would be required that night, and then there would be a briefing at which the target was announced. In his admirable study of 101 Squadron, *Bomber Squadron at War*, Andrew Brookes outlines what would then happen.

'Particulars would then be given of the *opposition* with crews being shown maps of where night fighters operated and where the flak, searchlight belts and barrage balloons were situated. A description of the landmarks by which the target could be found and the suggested lines of approach were then given, but these were only guidelines. Crews were given a great deal of latitude in the choice of routes to the target once the area in which it was located had been entered; after the briefing, captains and navigators would spend some time together working out the course that suited them best'.

This was a necessary freedom, for it was impossible to foretell the circumstances in which the attack would have to be made.

'Back in the briefing room the navigators, who were also the bomb-aimers, would then be issued with target maps. These maps were kept as simple as possible and were printed in various colours to represent woods, built-up areas, water and other easily distinguishable features. Photographs of the target were also shown to the crews and it was a wise bomb-aimer who studied these carefully because his memory and the simple map would be all he had to go on during the bombing run.'

As navigator and Flight Commander, Sandy Greig had a manifold responsibility although he was no longer asked to be bomb-aimer. In the spring of 1942, it had been decided that the title of 'observer' should be changed to that of 'navigator' and, more importantly, that an 'air bomber' should be added to the crew of heavy bombers like the Lancaster. The reason for this addition was simple, for there was concern about the navigator leaving his post some fifty miles from the target in order to concentrate on bomb-aiming. With the advent of Gee and other devices, it was felt that it was essential that the navigator should remain with his charts and black boxes throughout the operation.

The danger that faced air crews cannot be over emphasized. More were lost on their first six operational flights than at any other time of their careers. In the worst year, 1942, only three crews in ten could expect to survive their first tour, but this later 'improved' to the extent that a man had a fifty-fifty chance of living to the end of thirty operational missions.

By mid-1943, it had been decided that thirty operational missions in Bomber Command were as much as the bravest man could stand without running the risk of developing psychiatric illness. No man was officially allowed on operations once he had reached the age of forty. The findings of the RAF Medical Branch were responsible for these restrictions.

'A man subjected to prolonged or repeated fear due to battle stress will usually persist in fighting that fear as long as his supply of courage lasts. When his courage is exhausted he may either refuse to continue the struggle or develop a psychiatric illness if he has not already suffered death or injury at the hands of the enemy.'

It was the custom for a crew to be disbanded at the end of a tour of thirty missions and to be posted to training units where they would act as instructors whilst undergoing a period of recuperation for six months. They could then volunteer or be called back for a second tour of twenty operations. Only one man in four in Bomber Command survived two front-line tours, yet many — of whom Sandy Greig was one — volunteered to stay in operations on completion of their first tour rather than take the six months 'rest'. Those who survived their second tour could not again be ordered to fly on bomber operations.

Squadron Leader A.B.Greig, DSO, DFC, had completed his first tour with 218 Squadron and had moved immediately to his second tour with 101 Squadron, firstly as Squadron Navigation Officer and then as Flight Commander. He had flown more than his required number of missions on his second tour, and whatever his own wishes, it was the decision of the Royal Air Force that, in September 1943, he should cease to be air crew, but should join 28 Group pending posting to the Empire Air Navigation School in South Africa where his expertise and experience were to be used to the advantage of others.

While he was awaiting his posting he was asked by the BBC to give a talk entitled *Experiences over Turin*. It was understood that the talk was to follow the nine o'clock news, peak listening time during the war, and those at Ludford who were not flying that night listened eagerly; but there was no talk by Sandy. When he returned he told them that not only had the talk been transferred to BBC World Service, but that he had been handed a script which told him exactly what he had to say. That did not please Sandy Greig. Deception of any kind was not his way.

He had finished his tour before Scrym Wedderburn had finished his, but he managed to get back to the party his friend gave as a farewell to his air and ground crew. Inevitably, the party was held at the Royal Oak. The friends were not to meet again for many years, but when they finally came together, Mrs Scrymegeouw-Wedderburn was to remark to her husband that it seemed as if they had been meeting every day throughout the years they had been apart.

On 14 September 1943, Sandy Greig was posted to South Africa to begin another phase of his life.

In the years to come, he rarely spoke to his children about those years between 1939 and 1943. It would be untrue to say that he had not felt excitement and exhilaration, but he had seen a great deal of misery, so much death and destruction, and they were not things he wished to dwell upon in later years.

Few around him were to know of what he had accomplished other than the basic facts that he had been in 101 Squadron in Bomber Command and had won the DSO and DFC. In the Seventies, he and his wife flew to England for a special reunion dinner and she was surprised to find that they were seated on the top table. She asked the person next to her why this was so, and she was astonished to have the reply, 'Why! Didn't you know? This occasion is in your husband's honour.'

Sandy was perhaps the last to appreciate how deeply he had been scarred by the war. He had packed more into four years than most men do in a lifetime. He had flown over fifty missions in eighteen months, been wounded, received two awards for gallantry and seen many of his friends killed; and he was twenty-one years old.

The South African Connection

FROM early in the war it had been decided that trainee air crew should receive their basic flying training in the safety of an overseas posting. This was done under the auspices of the Empire Air Training Scheme, and Canada and South Africa were the most popular of training venues. Ken Farnes, for example, the England fast bowler, received his pilot training in Canada, only to be killed within four weeks of his return to England in October 1941.

This was the year in which the Ministry of Aviation issued a pamphlet describing the work of Bomber Command. The pamphlet distinguishes between the training given to the pilot of a fighter aircraft and the pilot of a bomber, and then goes on to say:

'The key man in the bomber aircraft is the navigator. His task is threefold. He must give his pilot the directions necessary to enable the bomber to reach the target at the right time; he must aim and release the bombs, and he must bring the aircraft and its crew safely back to base. Under ideal conditions his task is not difficult, but conditions are rarely ideal. Darkness, clouds, air currents, all singly or together, are his foes. His main preoccupation is with air currents for he finds himself, unless the wind is directly ahead or astern, in much the same predicament as a man trying to swim across a river disregarding the force of the current. It cannot be done. The speed and direction of the wind have to be calculated and taken into constant consideration throughout the flight.'

As we have noted, the navigator had been relieved

of the duty of bomb-aimer by the time Sandy Greig was posted to South Africa, and there was a constant advance in the development and use of technology. The navigator was still seen as the 'key man', however, and it is apparent why the Royal Air Force was so keen to use the expertise of Squadron Leader A.B.Greig in the training of others. He had survived two arduous tours, and a rest was now obligatory. Given the choice, he would have remained operational, but the Royal Air Force deemed that he should become an instructor in South Africa.

Although one may have dreams, it is hardly possible to make plans when one is flying bombing missions two nights in three and seeing friends and colleagues dying around one. Sandy Greig had no desire to follow in his father's business, nor to return to banking; and he certainly had no idea of settling in South Africa when he arrived there.

His initial impressions of the country were far from pleasant. At the beginning of December, he was taken to hospital with what was termed 'post-catarrhal jaundice'. The phrasing conveys jaundice that had been brought about by an infection that had attacked the liver, and it is possible that this was the first hint of a legacy from the heavy drinking in which he had indulged for over four years.

The illness took longer than expected to clear and it was mid-January 1944 before he was passed fit to report for duty.

Intelligent, firm and fair with a wealth of experience, he proved to be an outstanding instructor. It was not always easy in the sunshine and comfort of South Africa for young volunteers to anticipate what would be in store for them or how they would cope when they eventually came to active service. The inability to anticipate what lay ahead caused some to view the idea of extensive training as an annoying impediment in their eagerness to get into battle. Such young men received short shrift from Sandy Greig. He knew well the necessity of discipline and of mastering techniques. He knew, too, the price that one paid for lack of discipline and for ignorance of the job in hand, and he came down heavily on any who suggested a flippant approach to their training. The young trainees in Queenstown nicknamed him 'skipper'.

Once more he was offered a permanent commission, and once more he declined. The war had moved heavily in favour of the Allies, and Sandy's affection for South Africa had deepened.

He met a young lady named Josephine Emily Barry Taylor. She was a member of the Methodist Church of South Africa and one of a family of nine. She could match Sandy in strength of personality and in sporting prowess. On 8 December 1945, they were married at the Methodist Church, Manning Road, Durban, and, in spite of many trials and tribulations that lay ahead, they were to remain married until Sandy's death forty-five years later.

They set up home at 12 Livingstone Road, Queenstown, north of East London in Eastern Province. Sandy was officially released from the RAF in April 1946, but it was not until July 1959, that the *London Gazette* announced that his commission had been relinquished, but that he was to retain the rank of Squadron Leader.

A man of energy, enthusiasm and drive, when he left the RAF, Sandy Greig took a post in insurance with the Liverpool, London & Globe Company. For two years, he was backward and forward as, eminently successful at his job, he received several promotions.

Joyce, talented at several sports, was to become an excellent golfer at the Queenstown Golf Club and achieved a hole in one, a feat which was ever to elude Sandy, and she represented Border at both hockey and squash. Sport, family unity and discipline, commit-

31

Josephine Emily Barry Taylor, the girl who became Joyce Greig.

ment and a sensitivity to others were to be the guiding principles which were never violated.

Joyce and Sandy were to have four children, Tony, born in 1946; Molly Joy, born in 1949; Sally Ann, born in 1953; and Ian, born in 1955. All four were to follow the family principles and all four were to become involved with cricket, either directly or indirectly.

Molly had a highly successful marketing career. She was a buyer with a large firm in Cape Town and became the only female executive of the South African department store chain OK Bazaars. She worked for a time in the United States and set up her own business, but a broken marriage brought this to an end. Then she met and married N.O.Curry, who played cricket for Border in the Bowl Competition.

Curry is a university lecturer who, with Molly's help, has dedicated much of his life to assisting the cause of the black people in South Africa. They are a couple who value the dignity of human beings more than they value material possessions and he worked in Transkei and in other satellite states before taking up his present teaching post in Namibia.

Sally was to marry the Yorkshireman Philip Hodson, who headed the Cambridge University batting averages in 1973 and hit 111 against Kent at Fenner's. Tony and Ian were to play first-class cricket in England and for England, and of them, we shall speak more later.

Sandy and Joyce brought up a close and devoted family. Sandy was strict about schoolwork, about dress, behaviour and manners. He would give encouragement and praise where it was due and when it was needed, but he was never extravagant and he was always demanding that his children should keep their feet firmly on the ground and should be aware of the needs of others. He expected the four children to read the newspapers, especially the editorials, and he would ask their opinions.

It would be wrong to pretend that all was smooth

and easy. Sandy's rapid rise in the insurance business would have taken him to even greater heights if it had not been for his excessive drinking, a fallibility which most likely cost him the general managership of the Liverpool, London & Globe Company of South Africa. He was an alcoholic, something he never attempted to hide or excuse.

There is a tendency to believe that an alcoholic is somebody who is perpetually drunk. Sandy refuted this as a definition and insisted, with the wisdom born of painful experience, that an alcoholic is someone whose personality undergoes a significant change because of drink. He never offered his air crew service as an alibi or a reason for his alcoholism, but it is worth remembering that after the publication of the RAF Medical Branch's report on the likelihood of psychiatric illness for those engaged on their second tour of operations in Bomber Command, it became a standard joke in 101 Squadron and elsewhere that all they had to look forward to was 'coffin' or 'crackers'. By medical definition, Sandy had escaped both, but not all wounds and sicknesses are immediately visible or able to be diagnosed.

Joyce, strengthened by a Christian faith which never wavered, protected both her children and her husband, and Sandy never lost the position or dignity and respect which he held in her family as well as in his own. His nephews and nieces by marriage had a tremendous admiration for him because, despite his drinking habits, he was always so honest and straight. They knew exactly where they stood with him. They looked upon him as a mentor and they went to him with their problems, domestic or financial, and sought his advice. When there was a wedding or a family function, it was Sandy who was asked to preside as master of ceremonies. He was never to lose that sense of dignity, charm and authority which the Air Crew Selection Board had recognized.

His passion for sport never ceased. He played tennis, squash and golf, but it was as a coach and an administrator that he became so well known in South Africa. He ran the Swifts, the under-nineteen rugby side in Queenstown, and many of the young men who first learned the game under him went on to become top-class players. He was equally successful, and demanding, in cricket, and he became president of the Cricket Union in the area. As a player, he may never have achieved what he could have done at sport, but there are many who remain indebted to him for his ability as a coach and as an administrator.

The personal problem persisted and maintaining a responsible job was difficult. In 1967, he returned to Scotland. His father had remarried, but Sandy's step-mother had died. William Greig was now too old to run the family business and Sandy's half-brother, Ken, was too young. For a time it was thought that Sandy and Joyce would settle in Scotland, but in 1969, William Greig died. There was some confusion over the Bathgate business, and the A.B. branch of the Greig family returned to South Africa.

The problem was now, perhaps, more acute than ever as was the difficulty in holding a job. In 1970, Sandy began two years of special treatment in Northern Transvaal. For a time, all went well. He ran the library, worked on a book, read Robert Burns' poetry to his fellow patients nightly and his wisdom and learning made him the model student, but when he re-entered the mainstream of living he returned immediately to heavy drinking.

These were difficult times for the Greig family. Tony and Molly had left home, and the strain on Joyce must have been intense, but it was a period not without light. Tony was now playing first-class cricket in England, and Sandy had returned to Queenstown as editor of the *Daily Representative*. Queenstown was the smallest population centre in the southern hemisphere to have its own daily newspaper, and Sandy wrote every word of it.

It won a high reputation for its integrity and quality of writing, and there were those who learned much from it. One of them was Ken McEwan, the Essex batsman who delighted spectators throughout England in the late Seventies and early Eighties.

'Sandy was a very highly respected man in the Border area of the Eastern Cape who, together with his wife Joyce, brought up a very closely-knit family.

'I got to know him in my later school days when he reported schools cricket and rugby matches for the local paper in Queenstown. His knowledge of the sports, and fair praise and criticism, made him a well-respected journalist in the area, as would have been the case if he reported anywhere in the world.

'One of his reports has, and will remain with me for ever. It was during my last match for the school of which I was captain. We fielded first in what was a two-Saturdays match. The opposition made a huge total, and our bowling and fielding became very untidy. In his report on the Monday, he did not have too much praise for us, especially me for the way I handled the situation.

'Being an immature schoolboy, I took exception to this, together with my teammates. At the time, Ian happened to be my 'fag' at the school, and, typical of our immaturity, we made life very difficult for him during that week.

'The following Saturday, we batted, chasing about 280. We lost a couple of early wickets before I joined our opener. We had an unbroken partnership and won the game quite easily.

'In his report on the Monday, he praised us, especially me, but he reminded me of the previous week, again saying that my captaincy was bad and deserved criticism, but that I had made up for it, and he had given me just praise. Anyhow, Ian had a much more pleasant week at the boarding house.

'That incident has, and always will remain with me. Sandy taught me to accept the downs as well as the ups in life.'

Sandy, and the Greigs, certainly knew the downs as well as the ups. As editor of the *Daily Representative,* he continued to drink heavily, but it was a sudden illness rather than drink which caused a family crisis.

An intense pain in the abdomen was diagnosed as pancreatitis, and the surgeon offered the opinion that he would not last the night. Tony, playing in a Test match, and the other children were informed. It transpired that the afflication was a twist in the bowel, but this was not recognized until it erupted again when he was in Johannesburg.

It was here that he met up with an old newspaper colleague who took him to a clinic where the seeds were sown that were to lead him to give up drink. Sandy returned to Queenstown and called on the Presbyterian minister, telling him that he was intent on curing his alcoholism. Sandy, like the minister, knew that this was a job that he had to do himself. The minister had waited for Sandy to go to him. He knew that was how it had to be.

There was help at hand, however, in Dr Cliff Dent, the local veterinary surgeon, who had been along the same dark labyrinth as Sandy, and there were others in Alcoholics Anonymous who lent support. But in the end this is a battle which only the individual can win on his own, and in that respect Sandy Greig showed immense courage and an inner strength. It was more than a quarter of a century on, and he took every day as it came, but his war was over at last.

Throughout this time the church was most supportive. Joyce drew sustenance from the Methodist minister, Graham King, who has remained a family friend. She has always been a practising Christian, whereas Sandy found his own faith. In his own words, he made his peace with God and read his Bible, but he never felt the necessity to go to church. When he moved to Sydney, the local minister tried to persuade him otherwise, but Sandy remained adamant and the minister came to respect his ways.

He found a deep spiritual faith in Alcoholics Anonymous through the fellowship of other sufferers, and he came to give to that organization as much as he had learned from it. To the end of his life, he was ever ready to help others who wanted to overcome an alcoholic problem, but he always insisted that the only route to salvation was within each individual, however great the help from outside.

Throughout his time in South Africa, Sandy Greig had a reputation for fairness and straight-dealing that was never sullied. He did not differentiate between men because of the colour of their skins. He treated them as he found them, and he was respected by both blacks and whites, for he was a help to all, particularly on the sporting side. That the majority of white families in South Africa live a privileged existence is undeniable, and the Greigs were no exception, but the children were always made conscious of the fact that not all human beings were as fortunate as they were. They were also brought up to respect the innate dignity of all people.

The family servants, Sophie and her daughter, Nomketa, had their own premises and were an integral part of family life, but the Greig children were expected to look after themselves and to be self-sufficient to a great degree.

There was another member of the household who arrived uninvited one day and asked for a job. He had nothing but the khaki shorts and plimsolls which he was wearing, and although he could scarcely afford it, Sandy Greig gave the boy work as gardener. His name was Teki Manzi, although he was nicknamed

'Tackies', the name given in South Africa to the plimsolls that the boy was wearing.

Initially, there was no accommodation for him and a room was concocted for him out of part of the garage until special premises were built and he became a permanent part of the family. Officially employed as gardener and odd-job boy, he became fascinated by cricket. He would watch Tony at play with his schoolfriends, and soon he was allowed to join in. Never keen on batting, he was a lethal quick bowler with an illegal action, and he was to contribute much to Tony Greig's development as a cricketer, happily contributing hours as a net bowler. Sandy would sometimes complain that this was not what Teki Manzi was being paid for, but one feels that his complaints were never very serious and that he was content to see what was happening.

There was, of course, an ambivalence in Sandy Greig's position. He had married a South African and his children had been born in South Africa, but he remained defiantly British. There is, perhaps, not so much of a contradiction here. The manners and the standard of education that he found in South Africa in the Sixties and Seventies were very close to those that he had known and understood in Scotland in the Thirties. Fate, and the Royal Air Force, had planted him in South Africa. He had not chosen to go there, but in spite of all temptations to belong to other nations, he remained a Scotsman, and he later bore some resentment that his elder son had to 'qualify' to play cricket for the country for which he had fought.

If one lives one's life abroad, one does not cease to be British. Indeed, the distance from the homeland makes one more avid for news, more deeply concerned about what is happening in the land of one's birth. Living his rather solitary life in Russia, Guy Burgess confided to the actress Coral Browne when she visited him that the thing he missed most was the cricket scores.

Sandy never missed the cricket scores, nor the football and rugby results, and, like many who served in the Royal Air Force during the war, he held Dame Vera Lynn to be the greatest of singers and entertainers. In cricket, he held one man supreme above others, and that was an Australian, Donald Bradman.

In retrospect, we can see that there was some inevitability in Sandy Greig spending the last years of his life in Australia. His affection for Australians reached back to his days as a flight commander in 101 Squadron, when he found them the most loyal of companions and the best of men if, at times, infuriatingly ill-disciplined on the ground. There was an honesty about Australia, an energy and an openness of spirit which touched a chord in him and of which he approved.

Neither he nor Joyce had any intention of moving to Sydney, just as Sandy had never had any intention of settling in South Africa, but fate again played a part.

Tony's first-class career came to an end after his involvement with Kerry Packer's World Series Cricket in 1978-79. He settled in Sydney as managing director of a firm of insurance brokers and also pursued a career as a television commentator which, like so much else he did, was to revolutionize the game of cricket. In the world of business he had neither the experience nor expertise of his father.

Sandy had despaired of Tony's weakness in maths when his elder son was at Queen's College, and he had emphasized that a command of the subject was absolutely vital if one was to survive in business as an adult. A combination of school and parent and firm discipline improved Tony's maths considerably, but he would never rival his father's astute business brain. In Australia, he moved into a world of financial complexities and he was in need of advice and assistance. His father could supply both those needs,

Sandy and Joyce Greig, the parents of two budding young sportsmen.

and so Sandy and Joyce, like their four children, left South Africa.

Sandy would never have been a man to have stopped work. There was always something to be done, a problem to be solved, a transaction to be completed. In England, in 1989, he said that he must get home, for he knew that the insurance business in Australia was undergoing a difficult period and Tony had indicated that he needed some advice.

The Greigs quickly settled in Sydney. Sandy was never a stranger in any community in which he lived and within weeks he was a well-known and popular figure. Tall, upright, handsome and with a smartness which was never forbidding, he had a presence which was as indicative of wisdom as it was approachable. He was not given to levity, but he was a man of good humour. He was firm and resolute in discipline, but he was a man of great warmth.

In Sydney, he continued his work with Alcoholics Anonymous, and he would assist whoever asked for help. He was looked upon as a fountain of knowledge, a man whose opinions were worthy of respect and should be listened to. He had frequent visitors, notable among them was Bruce Francis, the former New South Wales, Essex and Australian opening batsman.

Francis was an old friend of the family, having known them in South Africa, and he would sit for hours and discuss politics and international affairs with particular reference to South Africa and the position of men like Mandela and Archbishop Tutu. Francis would store Sandy's opinions and relay them to Alan Jones, who would often quote them on his drive-time radio programme.

Sandy was not a well man. He suffered from emphysema, and if he had a fear, it was that he would slip into a decline with the loss of his physical capabilities. He was to be spared that. He was to end as a man, as he had always been.

With four friends, he became an institution in Sydney. Every Saturday morning they would meet in the Lord Dudley, a public house quite close to Sydney Cricket Ground. One was a former naval commander; one a financier; one an expert in food and wine; and one was Alan McGilvray, of whom Jack Pollard wrote, 'It would be hard for administrators of the Australian game to find a better advocate of sportsmanship and playing to the spirit of cricket'. Sandy and McGilvray were twin souls and good friends.

The five men occupied a corner of the bar each Saturday morning, always sitting in the same seats, always buying their own drinks. For Sandy, it was orange juice. They would sit for two hours, each acutely aware of what was happening in the world and of the consequences of what was happening, and they would talk over current affairs. The time, the place, the chairs were sacrosanct.

On Saturday, 17 November 1990, Sandy did not arrive for the weekly gathering. It was the first time in his five years in Australia, excepting the times that he had been on holiday in England, that Sandy had missed a Saturday morning meeting with his friends. He was to miss the following Saturday, too, and on Friday, 30 November, St Andrew's Day, his friends telephoned his house and learned that he had just died.

They met as usual on the Saturday morning. A frequenter of the bar attempted to sit in Sandy's usual chair, but the four prevented him. 'But he hasn't been here for two weeks,' the man complained. 'He's dead,' they said. 'No one's sitting in that seat today.'

It was a gesture that will be construed as sentimentality, but it was the only gesture that four veterans could make to one of their number. On Saturday, 8 December, Ian Greig sat in his father's seat before returning to England a few days later.

Ian had been put on alert by a telephone call from Tony some two days before his father's death, and he knew that when he next received a call from Australia it would mean that the end was very near. Sandy had seemingly recovered from an eye operation, but by the night of 28 November, he was on a life support machine. Surrey County Cricket Club gave Tony every assistance and he took the twenty-eight hour flight to Sydney, where he arrived not having slept for two nights. Yet it was the first time in twenty trips that he did not suffer the effects of jet lag.

Sandy Greig slipped away with the dignity and serenity that had been characteristic of his life. He had not always known peace within himself, but he had always maintained integrity. In preparing the family for the end, the doctor said, 'He's been there before. He knocked at the gates and came back, but now it is his time to go.' It is futile to say that he still had so much to do, so much to give. Had he lived to be 150, that would still have been the case.

What was astonishing was the effect that the news of his death had on casual friends and acquaintances. A young man who had lodged with Tony and who had sought advice from Sandy when he had financial problems, turned and ran from the house when he was told that Sandy was dead. On the Saturday, Ian went to the corner shop to buy wine and provisions for the gathering after the funeral. The shop was owned by a Cape-Coloured man who had left South Africa to seek his living in Australia. Naturally, he and Sandy had much to talk about.

'Are you having a party?' he asked Ian.

'No, a wake,' was the reply. 'The old man went yesterday.'

The shopkeeper broke down and wept.

The funeral attracted four times the number of people that had been expected, and the minister, Bruce Christian, who had been present at Sandy's death and who had argued with Sandy about his non-attendance at church, but who had come to understand his ways, conducted the service.

Tony's son, Mark, is leader of the drum majors at the Scots College, Sydney, and he headed a procession which included the pipes and drums as befits the passing of a Scottish soldier. Sandy Greig was laid to rest with the honour, dignity and reverence that were his due.

In spite, or perhaps because of his suffering and human fallibilities, Sandy Greig had the dignity and passion of the individual's creativity. He heard and touched the poetry of the earth which will be there as long as man is capable of perceiving the changing seasons. His greatest legacy was the passion, loyalty, honesty of purpose and inventiveness that was his gift to his family, and it is to them that we should now turn our attention.

Tony

TONY Greig was only thirty years old when his short, but brilliant career in Test and county cricket came to an end. It is some fourteen years since he stepped on a cricket field in England, yet the mention of his name still excites contradictory emotions and reactions. Like his father, he was born to lead, and the way of the leader and the innovator can be neither ever-smooth nor ever-popular.

The eldest of the four Greig children, he was born in Queenstown on 6 October 1946. Sport and a strong family discipline were an integral part of the fabric of his life. His education at Queen's College simply emphasized the principles and enthusiasms he imbibed at home. School was as much a feeder of his appetite for sport as it was a place of learning. The facilities for sport were excellent, and there was an abundance of staff dedicated to cricket, rugby and other sports and willing to give freely of their time.

Queen's has produced a string of rugby and cricket players of first-class quality, the most recent among them being the highly talented Cullinan brothers.

In all sports Tony Greig was a precocious talent. He was a Colossus in terms of physique and ability, and his influence on others was profound. He was appointed captain of the school rugby fifteen and revitalized an ailing side. He was captain of the tennis team and spent three years in the first eleven at cricket, being captain in his third year.

It was an environment in which he thrived. Queen's College rugby matches were frequently watched by crowds in excess of two thousand, and the cricket matches, too, attracted large crowds. They were all-day affairs, keenly contested.

A family Christmas. Tony and Ian with their parents and sisters Sally Ann and Molly Joy.

His school cricket was supplemented by cricket on the lawn at home where being the oldest and the tallest, he tended to dominate, using his brother and sisters as fielders while he batted. Molly Joy and Sally Ann were not so easily put upon, and the forceful Molly, the elder of the two, would often argue the women's point of view. There was also the support of his parents.

Sandy was a stern critic. He would rarely miss watching his son play, but he was never extravagant in his praise. He believed that feet should be kept firmly on the ground, and he would never allow Tony to forget errors he had made, even if those errors had not led to his dismissal. Tony had admitted that at the time he felt that he was treated too harshly, but

47

he came to understand and appreciate the value of the attitude his parents adopted. Joyce was always encouraging and gave praise, but she, too, was aware of the dangers that could be created by mothers and fathers who were too involved with their children, too uncritical.

Years later, as a father, Tony was to err on one occasion himself, but he quickly remembered the example of Joyce and Sandy, and he did not make the mistake again.

He was watching his son, Mark, in a rugby match and reacted strongly and verbally against a decision that the referee gave which went against his son. Later, the referee walked over to him and suggested that because of who he was, Tony could offer an opinion which others would follow, but that he, the referee, had concern for thirty boys, not one, and that he judged the game as he saw it. Tony's response was an immediate apology and the insistence that he buy a drink. Thereafter, he followed Sandy's maxims.

The quality of the cricket he was able to play at school was of tremendous benefit to Tony Greig. The side often travelled as much as two hundred miles to play matches and would journey overnight and be given hospitality by the parents of the opposing teams. As we have mentioned, games were played in front of large crowds, and from the age of fourteen or fifteen Tony was developing the temperament that was to stand him in such good stead when he came to play first-class cricket and lead England in Test matches. The competitive element in his game was innate.

Ken McEwan assesses the influence that Tony asserted. 'Tony was one of the biggest influences on my career. I recall, as a junior, watching the first eleven practise in the nets and dreaming of being there one day myself.

'Queen's is traditionally a good cricketing school, and at that time had some very good players. Every summer a professional was brought out from England to coach. They nearly always came from Sussex. Tony always stood out among the rest. He was always neatly turned out and very competitive, even in the nets.

'Soon after leaving school he joined Sussex, and I suppose because his father was the local reporter, all the county scores, especially Sussex, were published in the local paper. This all appealed to me and it was in those early years that I decided that all I ever wanted to do was to play cricket every day, for Sussex and South Africa.

'During my last year at school, Tony came back to Queen's in the English winter as coach. It was at this time that he arranged for me to spend a summer with Sussex. On looking back, I realize it was he who was responsible for opening a lot of doors for me, for which I will always be grateful.

'We were all influenced by Tony, and by the Greigs as a whole. One must not forget the part their mother especially, and their sisters have played in making them a happy, close-knit and most successful family.'

Tony's own successes, particularly on the cricket field, abounded. He was principally a hard-hitting batsman and a brisk medium-pace bowler, particularly effective because of his height, but he also demonstrated that he could bowl off-breaks if the occasion demanded, and it was a success in this area which brought him to the notice of the South African Schools' selectors.

While he was prospering on the sports field he was meeting with less success in the classroom, although he had decided that he wanted to be a teacher of history. He was accepted for a place at Rhodes University in Grahamstown and was offered a post at Queen's College as soon as he qualified. Unfortunately, at the end of the examination period, the equivalent of 'A' Levels, he went down with influenza. This caused him to miss the last two exams, but the school said that he could return and take them at the beginning of the following term.

He learned that he had passed all the examinations that he had taken, and the passage to university seemed smooth. It was then discovered that the school had been in error, and that it was necessary to pass in all subjects at one sitting in order to gain university entrance qualifications. At the second sitting, he failed Afrikaans, which had long been his Achilles' heel, and he was forced to return to school for another year and to study a completely different syllabus.

This frustration in his academic career was to prove fortunate for the cricket world. For the fourth year, he represented Border Schools in Nuffield Cricket Week.

Each year in South Africa, the schools representatives from some dozen areas gather to play a week's cricket. Caps, blazers and ties are presented to those chosen to represent their associations. They are accommodated in top-class hotels, and the matches receive wide Press coverage. The climax of the week is on the last day, when a selected national schools side plays against the senior side of the host province. The boys selected for this national side are awarded South African Schools blazers, which are held second in esteem only to the full Springbok blazer. The majority of South Africa's leading cricketers have graduated through Nuffield Week.

When Tony Greig was first selected for Border Schools in 1963 he was only sixteen years old and was competing against boys two and three years his senior. His first selection for the South African Schools side came in his third year, 1965, and then, he maintains, only because Mike Procter who had been the all-rounder in the eleven in the previous two seasons had upset the authorities in some way and was omitted as a punishment.

The host association was Griqualand West, and the

Schools XI beat them by 78 runs. Hylton Ackerman, later of Northamptonshire, captained the side, and Tony Greig batted at number six. He scored 23, held two catches and bowled five overs for four runs without taking a wicket.

The following season, 1965-66, not only was he an automatic selection for the Nuffield Schools XI, but he also made his first-class debut, appearing for Border against Transvaal 'B' in the last Bowl match of the year. He scored 37 in Border's first innings of 362, took two wickets, held two catches and saw his side win by six wickets and finish second in the competiton.

What was not known at this time, and what was not known until the close of Greig's first-class career and the publication of his book, *My Story*, in 1980, was that he had achieved his meteoric rise against the background of a disturbing medical report.

At the age of fourteen, playing tennis for Queen's College against Dale College, he had collapsed. At first, it was believed that he was simply suffering from exhaustion brought about by the excessive amount of training he was doing and the vast amount of sport he was playing. The family physician, Dr Sandy Voortman, was not satisfied that this was the reason, and Tony was sent to Cape Town to see a specialist at the Groote Schuur Hosptial.

The specialist diagnosed that Tony Greig was suffering from a form of epilepsy that would, in all probability, pass. The second part of his diagnosis was to prove untrue, for although attacks were not to be persistent, Tony Greig was never to be without threat of them. As a schoolboy, he was given a course of drugs and often tranquilized with an injection and kept in bed for anything up to a week.

A volatile and positive personality, Tony Greig refused to accept any of the restrictions that his disability should have placed upon him. He continued with his passionate dedication to sport, rejected protective moves and never mentioned his complaint throughout his cricket career, even though, on the occasion of his Currie Cup debut for Eastern Province, he suffered an attack while fielding at slip.

Paradoxically, Tony Greig's malady was influential in shaping his cricket career. Having qualified for univeristy, he expected to complete his year's compulsory National Service before taking up his place. The Army rejected him on medical grounds and although he was never given a reason for their rejection, it was assumed that it was on account on his epileptic history. He was now left with a year to fill before going to Rhodes University, and it was only on finding himself in this vacuum that he contemplated the idea of playing cricket in England.

There was a tradition of cricket coaches from Sussex at Queen's College, and in 1965-66, the man at Queen's was the all-rounder Mike Buss. Tony approached him and asked if there would be the possibility of spending a season with Sussex. It has recently become common for counties to provide opportunities in their second elevens for young cricketers from Australia, New Zealand and South Africa, but it was an infrequent occurence in 1966. Greig's school record was not outstanding, but he had won recognition both by the South African Schools' selection and, significantly, by the Border Association. Mike Buss recognized great potential and he lobbied hard for Greig. Sussex agreed to give him a year's trial at £15 a week providing that he paid his own fare to England.

The debt that Tony Greig, Sussex and English cricket owes to Mike Buss is enormous. An all-rounder who hit just under 12,000 runs and took 547 wickets in a career which spanned seventeen years, he was the ideal county cricketer. He began as a middle-order batsman and became an opener in 1966. He bowled both slow left-arm and medium-pace, and he was associated with Sussex during their vintage years in one-day cricket.

When he recommended Tony Greig to his county, he was still an uncapped player of twenty-two. It was a bold and brave move.

The problem that now faced Tony Greig was that of finding the money to pay for his fare to England. Sandy and Joyce were in no position to help at this time, but a family friend came to the rescue with a loan of £125 that would cover a single fare on the *Pendennis Castle*. Tony himself had to find work that would help supplement and repay this loan. For the three months before he was due to leave for England, he found employment with South African Railways in their diesel depot in East London.

His job was to sort and deliver letters and parcels in East London, and he was paid under £20 a week. It was a menial job and something of a shock for one who had enjoyed the somewhat privileged role as senior sportsman and student at Queen's College. He performed his task adequately, if without enthusiasm, but he received a fillip when an East London newspaper carried an article on him as a promising cricketer. This was read by his collegues at work who thereafter treated him as a celebrity and took much of his work load from him.

As the day of departure drew closer Tony suffered the feelings of apprehension that come to all young men in such circumstances, the fear of becoming a stranger in a strange land. Certainly his one ambition was to play cricket and to play for Sussex, but, confident and accomplished as he was as a sportsman, his life had been spent among a close-knit family and among people he knew. He now faced the prospect of no longer being a sporting giant, but a minnow in an alien society.

His worries were not eased when, only hours out on the *Pendennis Castle*, he and the other passengers were subjected to emergency regulations as one of their number had fallen overboard and had been drowned.

He journeyed to England with Mike Buss, less than three years his senior, but always called 'Sir' or 'Mr Buss'. The discipline of Queen's College was not easily shaken off, and he was still apprehensive about drinking or smoking, certainly in Buss' presence.

At Southampton, they were met by Mike Buss' elder brother, Tony, a fast medium-pace bowler and another Sussex stalwart, and by the county secretary, Colonel P.C. Williams. They were driven along the south coast to Brighton, on what was a cold and bleak day in late March, yet Tony Greig remembers well the first impression of the almost overpowering greenness of England. It is an intoxicant which has an immediate effect on all visiting the country for the first time or returning after a lengthy period abroad.

He was in good hands in Sussex. Not only did the Buss brothers see that he was well settled, but Alan Oakman, one of the senior professionals at Sussex and one who had coached at Queen's College, gave him a home for a fortnight until accommodation was ready for him. He was provided with a room at the house of Mrs Flo Cooper, a famous cricketing landlady. Mrs Cooper, who hails from Yorkshire, has provided comfort for many young Sussex cricketers in her home close to the Hove ground, offering a warmth and welcome that made life so much easier for young men just beginning their careers.

From the outset, Tony Greig impressed Sussex's experienced professionals with his dedication and competitiveness. In a wretched April, he was even seen practising his seam bowling on a carpet of snow, a deed which caused wise heads like Ken Suttle and Tony Buss to wonder at his sanity.

The Greig connection with Sussex was a strong one. One of Tony's earlier coaches at Queen's College had been Richard Langridge, whose career was drawing to a close when Tony arrived at Sussex. Richard had met and married a South African girl on one of his coaching visits to the Union. Margaret Langridge was a teacher, who had taught the Greig sisters. It had seemed that the lives of the Greigs and of Sussex County Cricket Club were intertwined, a supposition which only helped to reinforce Tony's determination to succeed.

He did well, if not spectacularly, in second-eleven cricket. Sussex won four of their first five games, then lost Foreman, Mike Buss and Graves to the first eleven and did not win again. Tony played 20 innings, scored 362 runs and averaged 22.62. He took 42 wickets at 21.24 runs each and finished third in the bowling averages. There were others, like Harry Newton, who could argue that they had at least done as well as Greig, but there was, and ever would be, a panache in Tony Greig's cricket that was infectious and appealing.

He played in several Sunday games that were staged for Ken Suttle's benefit, met the great players of the day and impressed with his attitude and enthusiasm in the field. When Sussex entertained Cambridge University at the beginning of July, he was one of three second-team players drafted into the side.

The University batted first. They had reached 85 for 4 before Tony brought about a collapse by taking three wickets in an over. He finished with 3 for 27 in 11 overs. Number eight on the card, he watched Mike Buss hit 136 before contributing a brisk 26 to Sussex's 372 for 9 declared.

His bowling met with no success when Cambridge batted again, and Sussex were left with ten minutes under three hours in which to score 133 to win. Greig came to the wicket with the score at 90 for 4 and, in the words of *Wisden*, 'emphasized his usefulness with an enterprising knock'.

He hit 25 not out, and Sussex won by five wickets. There were no other first-class appearances until the last day of August when fate again took a hand in his cricketing destiny.

The Hastings Festival began on Wednesday, 31 August with a match between Arthur Gilligan's XI and the West Indies touring team. Gilligan, a former captain of Sussex and England and an influential figure in the county, was restricted in his choice of a side as twelve of the seventeen counties were engaged in Championship matches. He had watched the progress of Greig with much interest and decided to include him in his side to play the West Indians, who had just won the Test series against England by three matches to one.

Unfortunately, rain prevented any play after the first day when the tourists made 351 and reduced Gilligan's men to 70 for 4. Tony Greig did not get to the wicket, but he bowled 16 overs and took the wickets of Kanhai, Nurse and Gibbs at a personal cost of 51 runs. It was an impressive performance, however light-hearted had been the West Indian approach to the game.

The reports of the match all spoke of Greig as being a 'young South African qualifying for Sussex'. This was not the case. He was still a young cricketer who was completing a year's trial. What was apparent was that his interest in resuming academic studies at university was waning. A season's cricket in England had excited a passion for the game which was already very very strong and which he now wished to pursue as a career.

He had done enough to convince the Sussex committee that he was an all-rounder of quality who could serve the county well, and at the end of the season he was offered a three-year contract which was to commence in 1967. By a thoughtful piece of administration, Sussex had cleverly anticipated that they might require the services of Greig, and, on 4 May 1966, at the beginning of his trial period, they had informed the Registration Committee of the Advisory County Cricket Committee that he had begun the required twenty-four months' residential period in order to be eligible to play for the county.

Having been offered a contract, Tony was still faced with the problem of convincing Sandy that he should become a professional cricketer rather than read for a history degree in Grahamstown. There can be little doubt that Sandy was immensely proud of his son's success and that he would be happy to see him following a sporting career, but his intitial response was cautious. He was unimpressed by the salary offered, and he was well aware of the uncertain future that would await a young cricketer whose performances did not come up to expectation and who had no qualifications to fall back on. He struck a bargain with his elder son. He gave him four years in which to make the grade as a top-class cricketer. If he failed to reach and maintain the necessary standard, he was to leave cricket and find a job which offered greater security. It was sound advice, and Tony both understood and appreciated it. Neither father nor son could imagine what the next four years were to bring.

Under the rules of residential qualification, Tony was allowed only two months' holiday during the winter period when he could leave Great Britain and visit his family in South Africa. He chose to take the Christmas period for his vacation, and the rest of the time he spent working in the family business in Scotland.

His grandfather employed him in the electrical department of the Bathgate store. William Greig, like his son Sandy, believed that young men should learn the disciplines of life, that if they were to be leaders, they must learn how to be led. Tony must begin at the bottom. He delivered, installed and collected television sets. He also had the unpleasant task of reclaiming sets when rent or payments were not met. It was a chastening balance to the heady days of cricket.

Being the grandson in the family business was not

without its compensations, and Tony was often allowed to borrow his grandfather's Daimler and drive amid the beauties of Scotland at weekends.

The return to South Africa for Christmas broke the work in Scotland and, as the cricket season drew nearer, there was the awareness that Tony Greig faced another year of mainly second-team cricket, for he would not be qualified for Sussex by residence until the beginning of the 1968 season.

In the early months of 1967, he appealed against the imposition of the two-year qualifying period under amendment to rule 5(d) which allowed a cricketer in his circumstances to serve only a one-year period of qualification. The appeal was upheld and Tony Greig was a Sussex cricketer, ready and eager to begin his first full season in the county game.

Sussex

SUSSEX have never won the County Championship, and when Tony Greig joined them in 1967 their period of dominance in the 60-over knock-out competition, the Gillette Cup, had just come to an end. The Nawab of Pataudi, who had captained the county in 1966, was leading India in 1967, and Jim Parks began a short and not altogether happy reign as captain.

Jim Parks' father, J.H., was the county coach, and Sussex was, and always had been, something of a family affair, with the Parks, the Langridges and the Oakes. The county was going through a difficult period with several players coming towards the end of their careers and others fighting to establish themselves. There were problems in leadership and administration. Between 1965 and 1969, Sussex had five different captains. It was not the ideal atmosphere in which a young player could be encouraged to thrive.

On Tony Greig, there was added pressure. He had been 'imported' by Mike Buss, and it was Mike, his brother Tony and Alan Oakman who were his staunchest supporters.

There are times when a county cricket club can be a place of intrigue. It is an intrigue born of insecurity. Only eleven players can take the field at a time; and the success of one man means demotion for another. The arrival of an outsider becomes an added threat.

There was considerable tension when the players reported back to the county headquarters at Hove on 1 April 1967, and speculation as to who would be able to establish themselves at the expense of some of the older players. Keenly competitive, Tony Greig was anxious not only to succeed on his own account, but to justify the faith that the Buss brothers had shown in him, a faith which was causing them some criticism and pressure.

Greig was always to respond well to pressure, and he displayed a sharpness in pre-season practise which few could rival. He was determined to force his way into the side and he received the confidence boost so necessary to a young player when, over a cup of coffee, skipper Jim Parks told him that he intended to give him a run in the side. He would bat at number five, and he was not to worry about low scores early on, for his place was assured for at least five or six games. He was being given a chance to settle.

There was no indication that he would be in the team from the outset, but he discovered that was the case when he was chosen for the first game of the season. Sussex were one of seven counties who had been drawn out of the hat to play in the first round of the Gillette Cup, and they had to travel to Worcester for the game on 29 April. Worcestershire had been finalists in 1966 and were a very strong side.

The pace bowling of John Snow and Tony Buss soon had them in disarray, however, and they were bowled out for 115 in 54.4 overs. Tony Greig did not take a wicket, but he bowled an admirably economic spell of ten overs for 11 runs. This was a remarkably mature performance by a young man who was confronting batsmen of the calibre of Ormrod, Graveney, D'Oliveira and Richardson for the first time.

Sussex's task seemed easy, but they slipped to 73 for 5, and it was only a determined batting display from Greig, joint top-scorer with 22, Griffith and Lewis that took them to victory by two wickets. It had been an impressive debut in a competitive match by the young all-rounder. His debut in the County Championship was to be even more impressive.

Sussex began their programme with a match against

Lancashire at Hove on 3, 4 and 5 May. Parks won the toss, and Oakman and Mike Buss went out to open the Sussex innings. Mike Buss was leg-before to Brian Statham at 9. Oakman was bowled by Ken Higgs at 17; and Jim Parks became another Statham victim at 34. At this point, Tony Greig came to the wicket for his first innings in a Championship match.

Statham was causing all sorts of problems bowling up the notorious Hove slope and aided by the sea fret. He hit Greig on the foot, but his appeal for leg-before was rejected. Gathering confidence and concentration, Tony Greig reached his half-century and then began to show a wide range of shots. In spite of some hesitancy in the nineties, he reached his century in three hours and added another 56 in less than another hour. He was out when he heaved at Savage, missed and was leg-before.

He had taken Sussex from the dangers of 34 for 3 to a total of 324. The next highest score was Graves' 32 in a fifth-wicket stand of 117.

John Snow reduced Lancashire to 21 for 4 by the close, and, as it transpired, that was the end of the match, for rain prevented any play on the second and third days.

Greig's innings included 22 fours, and it captured all the cricket headlines. *The Cricketer* hailed him as one of the men of the moment, pictured him on the cover and talked of the innings as exceptional. It also suggested that he had tried to gain admittance to Fitzwilliam College, Cambridge, but was to take a three-year course in physical education at Brighton College. These statements were untrue, but it was correct that a 'meteor had arisen'.

It was not simply the quality of this maiden century that attracted attention, but the build and personality of the cricketer himself. He stood six feet seven and a half inches tall, and there were very few people whom he did not smile down upon. His blond hair would gleam in the sun, and a striking physical presence served to mirror the strength and dynamism of the personality. He had the aura which left one in no doubt as to his ability and his commitment. He was dedicated and fiercely competitive, yet off the field there was a gentleness of manner, a product of his parents and of his education at Queen's College.

His dashing century against Lancashire gained him instant recognition and was followed by the inevitable corrective. None had been more pleased about his century than the Buss brothers, who were now proved to be right in their judgements, but they, and Alan Oakman, were able to smile at what happened next. Sussex travelled to Cambridge to play the University at Fenner's. Cooper for Tony Buss was the only change from the side that drew with Lancashire. The University were bowled out for 91 and 95, but Greig failed to take a wicket.

There was a sizeable crowd at Fenner's, many, no doubt, having gone to see the new star. He came to the wicket with the score on 64 for 3 to face the bowling of off-spinner David Acfield. The ball pitched outside off stump. Greig essayed an extravagant cover-drive and his middle stump went back. It was a salutory lesson, and it was not forgotten.

When he arrived back in the Sussex dressing-room he was immediately enrolled into the Primary Club by Alan Oakman. The Primary Club is open to all those who, at one time or another, have been dismissed first ball. In 1967, membership cost a guinea, and then, as now, you received a tie. The money raised by this worthy club goes to providing facilities for the playing of the game by blind and partially-sighted cricketers.

Sussex went on to beat Cambridge University by nine wickets, and then it was back to the more serious business of the County Championship. At Brentwood, Essex were set to make 179 in less than two hours and got in dreadful trouble against Snow, Greig and

Tony Buss. They were 8 for 4 and ended on 74 for 7, saved only by the durable Trevor Bailey. Greig's figures were 3 for 28. Keith Fletcher had provided him with his first wickets in Championship cricket, and Brian Taylor with his first catch.

Victory over Middlesex at Hove took Sussex into the quarter-finals of the Gillette Cup, and then Glamorgan were beaten in the Championship match at Hove, although Tony contributed little to the victory. There followed four drawn Championship matches, including the traditional Whitsun Bank Holiday game with Middlesex at Lord's which was ruined by rain, in which Greig had his worst run of the season. The euphoria that had accompanied the innings against Lancashire was fading from memory, and there were suggestions that the innings had been no more than the fortune which often attends a beginner.

The turning point came in the local derby with Hampshire at the beginning of June. The Hove pitch favoured the seam bowlers, and Parks asked Hampshire to bat first. Greig took 4 for 34, including the last three without conceding a run, and the visitors were bowled out for 206. Sussex just edged into a first-innings lead, despite the bowling of Shackleton, and the match became a one-innings contest. At 52 for 3, and the wicket seemingly becoming easier, Hampshire were moving towards a winning position, but Tony Greig turned the course of the game completely with a devastating spell which brought him 6 for 16 in 11 overs.

There was victory over Warwickshire, with Greig hitting 64, and he followed this with 62 and five wickets at The Oval where Sussex were beaten for the first time that season. There was quick compensation for this in the quarter-final of the Gillette Cup.

Their opponents were Hampshire, and the Hove ground was full to capacity with 10,000 people. At 152 for 5, Sussex desperately needed quick runs as their overs were running out. Greig hit a brisk 46, the highest score of the innings, and Sussex reached 233 for 9. This was hardly a winning total, particularly as Snow had lost direction and was hit for 59 in 11 overs, whilst Suttle went for 65 in his 11. Greig and Bates bowled Sussex back into contention. Greig took 2 for 26 in 12 overs, sending down five maidens at a crucial time, and Sussex won a thrilling game by nine runs. Tony Greig was named man-of-the-match for the first time.

The elation continued. Against Gloucestershire at Hove, Ken Suttle hit 138 to take Sussex to a first-innings lead, and then Greig swung the game irreversibly in Sussex's direction by taking 8 for 25, the last six wickets while conceding only two runs. In statistical terms, this was to remain the best performance of his career.

Sussex were now fourth in the Championship table and into the semi-final of the Gillette Cup. A week later, at Bristol, Tony Greig hit 55 and 123 against Gloucestershire, but there followed a crashing defeat at the hands of Kent in the Gillette Cup semi-final, and Sussex went into a decline from which they never recovered. They finished thirteenth in the Championship table, a bitter disappointment. Their sole consolation was that they had scored their runs more quickly than any other county.

For Tony Greig, the first season had been one of triumph. He hit 1,299 runs, took 67 wickets, and, like his colleague Mike Buss, was awarded his county cap. He was voted as Young Cricketer of the Year by the Cricket Writers' Club. It was a formidable start to a county career.

He was not to return to South Africa in the winter of 1967-68, for the Greig family were now in Scotland. Sandy had brought them to Bathgate as he took over the running of the business from his ailing father. As we related earlier, they were only to remain there for two years, but it was a support and a comfort for Tony at this time.

His cricket career was to be further enriched when he was invited by the late Joe Lister to join the International party that was to tour Africa and Asia. It was a three-month tour comprising twenty-one matches, four of which were first-class. The trip involved some 32,000 miles of air travel, but the side was undefeated, winning 15 of their matches.

There were some outstanding cricketers in the party which was captained by Mickey Stewart. Amiss, Denness, Fletcher and Underwood, all of whom were to become closely associated with Greig in the next few years, were among the fourteen.

Greig's bowling was far too good for the cricketers of Sierra Leone, and in Karachi, against a strong Pakistan Board of Control XI, he and Fletcher added 130 in under two hours in the second innings. Before a large crowd in Madras, Tony Greig reached the third first-class century of his career, and he and Billy Ibadulla put on 96 in 92 minutes for the fifth wicket. After Greig had been bowled by Kumar for 106, it was discovered that he had been batting with a broken bone in his right hand. Joe Lister offered him the chance to fly back to England, but he decided to remain with the side, although he was to take no further part in the tour. It was this feeling for team unity which was later to make him such a popular captain.

The plaster that had to be placed on his broken hand was removed in time for him to join the rest of the Sussex side in training at the beginning of April 1968, but he had been very active in other directions before then.

When he received the invitation to tour Africa and Asia with the International side, Tony Greig realized that his South African passport would be a liability and that he was likely to be refused entry into several countries. He approached the South African embassy and told them of his intention of applying for a British passport. They refused to condone any hint of a change of nationalities and even suggested that they would withdraw his citizenship. He felt that he had no option but to go ahead with his plan and wrote to the South African Minister of the Interior and explained his position. The Government relented and gave him official permission to apply for a British passport. His application was immediately successful so that he was now a holder of two passports.

This led Sussex to make further approaches to the Registration Committee with regard to Greig's status. They asked that he should be recognized as English-born, offering in support of their claim that he was the holder of a British passport permanently resident in the United Kingdom and that his father was a British subject who had served in the war and was now running a family business in Scotland. The committee rejected the appeal and stated that, as Greig had been born in South Africa, he could not be considered an English-born cricketer until he had resided in the United Kingdom for five years as required by rule 7(d). That was not the end of the saga.

After the euphoria of his first Championship season and of the tour with the International side, Greig's second season was to prove most disappointing. His own form gave satisfaction, if not elation, with more runs, 1,305, than he had hit in 1967, at a better average, 26.10. His bowling was not quite so successful, his 55 wickets costing more than 35 runs each, but he was once again outstanding in the field, holding 28 catches, one less than he had taken in 1967.

If these figures suggest satisfactory progress or consolidation, the same could not be said for Sussex, who finished bottom of the County Championship for only the second time in 72 years. This was a sad time for the county. There was failure on the field and discontent both on and off. The politics of cricket can be painful, and in Sussex, they were compounded by a generation gap. As *Wisden* commented: 'The passing years cannot have helped towards producing sustained effort. Eight of the nineteen players included in the Championship programme were on the wrong side of thirty and though the recall of the thirty-seven-year-old Marlar for two matches had a nostalgic ring about it, the move did nothing to help.'

Ted Dexter was also recalled for two matches at the request of the England selectors, who then called upon him to reappear for his country. Dexter was thirty-three years old and had decided to retire from cricket, but he hit 203 against Kent at Hastings on his return, an innings which Greig considered to be a masterpiece. He also believed that Dexter's mere presence in the side made Sussex feel like a team again, but this was mid-July, and by then wounds had begun to fester.

At the beginning of the season, under the leadership of Jim Parks, the county won only one Championship match. Parks was bitterly disappointed with his own form and found it hard to maintain discipline and morale. There was a sterner, more relentless approach to the game by the younger players which the elder statesman, reared in an age when winning was less important than it is today, found difficult to understand. Not only was there a gap between players in the side in age and attitude, there was a chasm between the players and the administration. At the beginning of July, Parks resigned the captaincy.

The majority of the players would have chosen Tony Buss as his successor. He was a determined, experienced and successful county professional of twenty-eight. Even in this dreadful year of 1968, he was one of the few men to have maintained form, but the committee named Mike Griffith as the man to take over from Parks.

The distinction between amateur and professional was five years in the past, but pedigree and tradition were still dear to many in power on the south coast. Mike Griffith was the son of 'Billy' Griffith, a former captain of Sussex and, at the time, secretary of MCC. He was a Cambridge blue, a good wicketkeeper and a fine fielder as well as a batsman for whom the greatest of futures was predicted. The prophecy was not to be fulfilled. As his career progressed, it seemed that his cricket went into decline. In 1968, he was twenty-four years old and far from ready to be captain of a side that was full of discord. Greig, still a novice in the first-class game, had no understanding of the politics and liked Mike Griffith as a man, but he knew he was not the player to captain Sussex in 1968.

Alan Hill was to write later of Griffith in his book *The Family Fortune*: 'He lacked the strength of character to be a successful leader; by his own admission he was inclined to be flippant and casual in his approach to people; and the personality handicap meant that he floundered in his attempts to knit together an admittedly disunited team.'

There were compensations. As Hill observed, 'Mike Griffith, like other university contemporaries, stumbled on the bridge between amateurism and professionalism. He did not suffer from the inhibitions of many of his fellow players; he was able to enjoy cricket because the stakes were not so high for him. The zest and urgency of his play was tailor-made for the one-day game, where he delighted in improvised stroke-play and was a brisk and alert runner between the wickets.'

His penchant for the one-day game came close to salvaging something from his disastrous first half season as captain.

At the end of May, Sussex trounced Derbyshire by ten wickets at Hove in the second round of the Gillette Cup. Tony Greig took three wickets in six balls and finished with 4 for 28 as the visitors were bowled out for 97. It was a performance which gained him the individual award.

In the quarter-finals, the batting of Suttle and Dexter

earned a seven-run win over Northamptonshire; and by the time that the semi-final against Gloucestershire arrived, Griffith had taken over the leadership from Parks. This game was spread over three days because of the weather, and Sussex, batting first, reached 219 thanks to substantial contributions from Dexter, Greig, Parks and Cooper. This was a total that Gloucestershire never looked like matching, and Sussex were again in the Final of the competition which they had relished since its inception in 1963. Their opponents were Warwickshire, who had won the trophy in 1966.

Without Cartwright and Bannister, the Warwickshire attack looked decidedly weak, and Oakman and Mike Buss gave Sussex a sound start with a stand of 54. It ended when Oakman, playing his last game for Sussex, was caught behind off a leg-glance by the diving Alan Smith. By lunch, Sussex were 85 for 4 off 31 overs, and with Suttle and Dexter two of the departed batsmen, the game was very much in favour of Warwickshire.

After lunch, Greig and Parks tilted the game in Sussex's direction as they added 78 in 21 overs. Amiss, pressed into service to bowl left-arm medium pace, was particularly severely dealt with in what Christopher Martin-Jenkins described as 'a memorable period with a rich variety of strokes'.

Sussex made 214 for 7 from their 60 overs and when they reduced Warwickshire to 155 for 6 in 47 overs, the game seemed to be theirs. Alan Smith, the Warwickshire captain, believed otherwise. He took the attack to Sussex, and he and Amiss scored the 60 runs needed for victory in ten overs. Smith was twice dropped, and Sussex wilted in the field.

Jim Swanton described it as the best day's cricket of the season, and Richie Benaud considered it to be the best day's cricket he had seen for some years. Tony Greig smouldered that Sussex had lost a game that they should have won.

There was not even the consolation of an appearance in the Gillette Cup Final in 1969. Sussex reached the semi-finals where they were overwhelmed by Derbyshire at Chesterfield, finished bottom of the inaugural John Player Sunday League and, after a dreadful start to the season, climbed to a welcome seventh in the Championship. Greig's contributions were much as they had been in his first two seasons except that his bowling showed a marked improvement with 69 wickets at 23.60 runs each.

None of this could hide the continuing unrest within the county. Fast bowler Allan Arthur Jones, who was to become the first cricketer since the introduction of qualification regulations to play for four counties, left in mid-season as a protest against selection policies. Racionzer was another who decided that he was not enjoying cricket at Sussex and would go elsewhere. Snow could never seem to rouse himself to play for Sussex with the verve and aggression that he showed for England. He was later to confess that the county game was an anticlimax to him after Test cricket.

On the administrative side, Sussex had failed to sign Barry Richards because Hampshire offered him a salary that the Sussex committee refused to match. The South African batsman, considered the best in the world at the time, was also said to be reluctant to join Sussex because of the rumbles of discontent of which he had become aware. Griffith's position was unenviable. There was a lack of discipline which bordered on anarchy.

The pattern was unaltered in 1970. Again Sussex were bottom of the John Player League, saved only from total ignominy by winning two of their last three games and having the other abandoned. In the Championship, in an uneven season, they were ninth. Their best cricket was once more to be seen in the Gillette Cup where Tony Greig took the man-of-the-match award for an all-round performance which helped beat Kent by 47 runs in the quarter-final. He hit 54 out of 199 and came on to bowl with Kent 88 for 1 in the 35th over, seemingly cruising to victory. He took five of the last seven wickets for 42 runs. The Final saw Lancashire beat Sussex with some ease.

There was a tedium of mediocrity and lack of joy and purpose in much of Sussex's cricket. They tended to reduce others to their level, and they were often dull to watch, lacking in leadership, unity and direction.

For Tony Greig, there was lightness amid the gloom. By the end of the 1970 season, he was an England cricketer.

. . .and England

MANY players are gifted; few are able to pursue their careers with such a relentless passion as Tony Greig brought to the game. Dedicated and enthusiastic, he applied himself with a restless energy that could exhaust those around him. Whatever rewards he was to receive in later life, they were as much the fruits of hard work as of natural talent. He was unsparing of himself.

At the end of the 1968 season in England, he returned to Queen's College as coach, so maintaining the Sussex tradition at Queen's. He was welcomed back as a hero, but he proved a hard and determined task master. His attitude was both respected and appreciated.

He was able to assist Border in the 'B' Section of the Currie Cup. This was later to become the Bowl competition. Border had first introduced Greig to first-class cricket and he now rewarded them with some excellent performances. The side was unbeaten in the six matches of the campaign and finished second to Western Province. Tony Greig's contributions were significant.

He bowled Border to victory over Natal 'B' in East London, hit a dashing 94 which brought first-innings points against Transvaal 'B' in Johannesburg and took ten wickets in the match, 4 for 52 and 6 for 65, as Orange Free State were beaten by nine wickets. He ended the season as Border's leading wicket-taker with 25 wickets.

It was an important period for him. He was both teaching and playing, and he was learning through both experiences. He was also testing his skills against players of the quality of the Pollock brothers and Eddie

Barlow, and his own game was being honed and refined.

He was coach for a term at Queen's College the following season and again assisted Border. Figures of 10 for 84 in the final match against North-Eastern Transvaal in East London brought his total of wickets to nineteen in four matches. His success in South Africa was always to be more with the ball than with the bat.

He spent only a term in Queenstown because he had accepted an invitation to tour the Caribbean with the Duke of Norfolk's side. There were thirteen in the party which was captained by Colin Cowdrey. The Duke managed the side himself, and he had E.W.Swanton with him as treasurer and Charlie Elliott as umpire. Greig played in all three first-class matches, averaged 36.25 with the bat and took four wickets at 26.75 runs each. It was his first experience of cricket in the Caribbean, and he was continuing his varied and stimulating apprenticeship, and he was becoming a better and wiser cricketer.

He looked forward to the summer of 1970 and to the visit of the South African side to England. The South Africans were, at that time, the finest side in the world without question. They had just beaten Australia by four matches to nil in a four-match series. Their lowest margin of victory had been by 170 runs in the First Test.

The South African tour of England in 1970 did not take place. The campaign against apartheid in South Africa had gained tremendous support internationally, and the threat to disrupt matches in which the South Africans took part could not be ignored. The Government advised that the tour should be cancelled and the TCCB very reluctantly agreed. The cancellation was to signal the end of South Africa's participation in Test cricket, an isolation which only now looks like being ended.

To compensate for the cancellation of the South African Test series, the TCCB arranged five matches against a strong Rest of the World side which, ironically, included five South Africans — the Pollock brothers, Barry Richards, Eddie Barlow and Mike Procter. Norman Preston, then editor of *Wisden*, accorded the matches Test status, but that accreditation has discreetly been allowed to lapse over the years. The public stayed away in their thousands, particularly after England lost the first match by an innings, but the series was not without its value.

England were able to blood several players in international cricket. Among them was the luckless Alan Jones of Glamorgan, who appeared in the first game of the series, made 5 and 0, and was never given another chance at 'Test' level in the rest of an illustrious career. For the second game, England brought in Tony Greig.

It is questionable whether his form at the time justified his selection, for he was playing in a poor county side, but his very presence on a cricket field had an electrifying effect on those who saw him. He was an urgent, busy cricketer, ever making a contribution either with the bat, ball or in the field, often in all three areas. He certainly made his mark on his international debut against the Rest of the World at Trent Bridge in July 1970.

The Rest of the World had won the first match of the series by an innings and 80 runs, and England made five changes for the second match. Greig was the only new cap and he was quick to make an impression as he captured the wickets of Barry Richards, Kanhai, Sobers and Engineer at a personal cost of 59 runs when the Rest of the World were bowled out for 276 on the opening day. He scored 14 and England led by three runs on the first innings.

The Rest of the World made 286 in their second innings, and Greig bowled Richards and Barlow and had Sobers caught behind. To dismiss the two greatest batsmen in the world twice on the occasion of one's international debut was a remarkable achievement and Tony Greig could be well pleased with his match figures of 7 for 114 as England went on to win by eight wickets.

He had no success with the ball in his second match, but he hit 55 and 22 and held two catches. His versatility in the field — he was sharp in close-catching positions and at slip and athletic in the outfield — was to remain a great asset to any side for whom he played.

At Headingley, he was again among the wickets, claiming Barlow, Mushtaq Mohammed, Graeme Pollock and Intikhab Alam for 86 runs in 31 overs, yet he was omitted from the England side for the last match of the series. More surprisingly, he was not named in the England party to tour Australia the following winter. This was a great disappointment and his omission was roundly condemned in the Press.

The Cricketer was convinced that he had 'proved himself a Test player at Trent Bridge', and Jim Swanton's response to the chosen party was to say that the inclusion of Greig and Robin Hobbs would have transformed what looked to be a poor fielding side. Greig had topped the England bowling averages in the matches against the Rest of the World, his eleven wickets costing 26.18 runs apiece. Batting low in the order, he had averaged only 19.20.

Disappointed as he was at not being selected for the tour of Australia, Greig was consoled by the fact that the bargain that he had made with Sandy had been fulfilled. Within four seasons he had graduated from county professional to England player capable of holding his own with the best in the world.

Nevertheless, Ray Illingworth took the England side off to Australia and triumph while Tony Greig went to South Africa and played for Eastern Province.

Border had encouraged him well, but it was obvious

Tony Greig bowling for England.

that he now needed the stronger challenge of the 'A' Section of the Currie Cup with men like Bacher, Bland, Irvine, van der Byl and Rice, and that could only be provided by assisting Eastern Province.

Tony Greig's debut for Eastern Province was unforgettable, not in the playing sense, but for an incident to which we have already made some reference. The match was on the Wanderers Ground in Johannesburg, and Eastern Province were to meet the mighty Transvaal. The Eastern Province side, which was captained by Peter Pollock and included Graeme Pollock, Bland, Biggs and Wilmot, arrived for practise at the Wanderers on the afternoon before the game. Greig was thrilled by the prospect of playing among such noted company, men whom he had admired since he was a pupil at Queen's College, and, in his state of high excitement, went out for a meal and a few drinks when he would have done better to have gone to bed. He returned to his hotel feeling giddy, but he went to bed determined that nothing would prevent him from playing the next day.

When he awoke he felt worse than he had done the night before and collapsed. A doctor advised him not to play, but the determination which was to make him a great cricketer on the one hand and, occasionally, a stubborn individual on the other, asserted itself. He insisted that he would take his place in the side.

Transvaal won the toss, and Bacher and Bath opened the batting against Peter Pollock and Schmidt. There were twenty runs on the board when Bath edged Schmidt to slip where Greig held the catch with ease. Nineteen runs later, Carlstein was out in the same manner, and Tony Greig had made an auspicious start. He was to contribute little more to the match. Shortly after Ali Bacher had been run out, Greig slumped forward at slip and it was immediately apparent to Peter Pollock and to others that he was suffering an epileptic fit. Ali Bacher, a doctor by profession, ran on to the field and gave him an injection. After some minutes, Greig was carried from the field unconscious and it was reported that he was suffering from sunstroke. The astonishing fact is that this was the only attack he was to suffer on the cricket field, and he was to keep secret his afflication from Press, public and many of his administrators and colleagues in the game, until he chose to reveal it in 1980.

He insisted on returning to the match with Transvaal on the third day, by which time Ali Bacher and Lee Irvine were engaged in an unbroken stand of 205, aided by the fact that Scmidt and Peter Pollock, as well as Greig, had been unfit to bowl. Tony did, in fact, send down seven overs, and he hit 28, second-highest score, in Eastern Province's second innings, but his side were well beaten.

He blamed himself for the attack he had suffered on the opening day at the Wanderers Ground, believing that it was his own lack of discipline in preparing for the match which had caused it. He was to adopt a more responsible approach ever afterwards, but one must admire the man's insistence that he would not allow his condition to hinder his determination to reach the highest standards in cricket.

To Eastern Province, he remained eternally grateful. The seizure which Tony had suffered against Transvaal was as troubling to his colleagues as it was to Tony himself, but there was never a suggestion that he should not return to the side in case it happened again. He responded with 73 in the next match, against Natal, but it proved to be his highest score of a poor season. Much had been expected of him and nine wickets at more than 55 runs each and 147 runs, average 16.33, was a very disappointing return.

Possibly, it was the attack in Johannesburg which affected his later form; possibly, it was because he was preoccupied by his marriage to Donna Reed which took place in March 1971.

Donna was a friend of Molly Greig's, and Tony had known her since his schooldays in Queenstown where the Reed family also lived. Tony and Donna were to have two children, Samantha and Mark.

The newly-wed Greigs arrived back in England in April 1971, with Tony eager to establish himself in the England side and confident that he could do so. He was to be disappointed once again, although he gave yeoman service to Sussex who continued to suffer traumas.

Most of their problems revolved around John Snow, whose fast bowling had done so much to help England win the Ashes in Australia the previous winter. He seemed more than disenchanted with the county game, and after he had taken only three wickets for 223 runs, he was dropped from the Sussex side. Secretary Arthur Dumbrell issued a statement in which he said that Snow's 'bowling performances, and more especially his fielding, have been so lacking in effort that the selection committee had no alternative. Whilst recognizing the great physical strain of bowling fast, they felt that John Snow's indifferent attitude, if left unchecked, would jeopardize the morale of the rest of the side.'

Snow's problems did not end there. He was recalled after a month and returned to the England side for the First Test against India at Lord's. India were the second tourists of the summer. At the start of the Indian second innings, Gavaskar attempted to take a quick single and was barged to the ground by Snow as the pair ran up the pitch together. Snow was requested to apologize, which he did, but he was still omitted from the next Test as a disciplinary measure.

All this hardly helped a Sussex side for whom internal strife now seemed an accepted part of life. Victories late in the season lifted them to eleventh in the Championship, but in spite of persuading Ted Dexter to play in fifteen Sunday League matches, they finished no higher than seventh in that competition.

They did not even enjoy their usual compensation, being well beaten by Gloucestershire in the first round of the Gillette Cup.

From this debris, Tony Greig emerged with his reputation enhanced. The initial lethargy and subsequent absence of John Snow threw more work on to Greig's shoulders. He bowled more than 700 overs in the Championship alone and finished top of the county averages with 71 Championship wickets at 28.18 runs each. He hit two centuries, scored well over a thousand runs and held 31 catches, yet he could find no place in the England side throughout the summer. He was playing better than he had been in 1970 when chosen to play against the Rest of the World, but it was Richard Hutton who was given the all-rounder's spot in two Test matches against Pakistan and all three against India. Hutton was four years senior to Greig, but he had not previously been seen as a serious rival to the Sussex all-rounder who, if disappointed, showed no sign of relaxing his determination to become a Test cricketer.

Although he had not been selected for the England side in 1971, he was to receive a most welcome boost to his career, one which was to prove the turning point that led him on to success at the very highest level.

South Africa were scheduled to tour Australia in 1972-73, but sustained political and moral pressures led to its cancellation. As in England in 1970, it was replaced by a series between the home country and A World XI. Four English county players, Norman Gifford, Bob Taylor, Richard Hutton and Tony Greig, were invited to tour with the World side which was captained by Gary Sobers. Of the four English players, only Greig was selected to appear in all five representative matches. He was an outstanding success.

He was opposed by a wealth of emerging talent, men like Dennis Lillee, Rodney Marsh and the Chappell brothers with whom he was to become closely acquainted over the next few years, and from the beginning of the tour, he impressed everyone. The World XI took the series by two matches to one. Greig averaged 30 with the bat and played a significant part in his side's two victories.

In the third match, at Melbourne, he came to the wicket with the score at 26 for 4 and hit 66. He then took 4 for 41. Sobers followed with a memorable innings of 254 and, having trailed by 101 on the first innings, the World XI went on to win by 96 runs. At Adelaide, in the deciding game, Greig had six first-innings wickets for 30. He topped the bowling averages in the representative matches and for the tour, and in batting, only Sobers, Kanhai, Graeme Pollock and Clive Lloyd stood ahead of him. He was, as *Wisden* reported, 'a conspicuous success'.

Before he had set out on this tour, Tony had met with his father who told him that in Australia he was likely to meet a man who would talk to him about cricket. Sandy insisted that if that man, Don Bradman, spoke for six hours and said only one thing of note or offered only one piece of advice, that single statement could alter the future of his career and must be imbibed. Certainly, Tony met Bradman; and certainly he was a far better player at the end of the tour than he was before it started.

He flew directly from Australia to South Africa, and within hours of landing he was playing for Eastern Province against Western Province at Newlands in Cape Town. He had agreed to play for Eastern Province in the later stages of their Currie Cup campaign and began by taking 5 for 39 in 26 overs. It was the start of an exciting spell. In four matches for Eastern Province, he took 25 wickets at 13.32 runs apiece. He was mature in attitude and performance, dominant and assured without ever being complacent. Wrote Geoffrey Chettle: 'For the first time in South Africa, Tony really revealed his true overseas form'. He was named as one of South Africa's Five Cricketers of the Year.

Therein lay the rub. Although seen by some in South Africa as a 'foreigner' or a 'deserter', he was still considered by some in England as an outsider, an overseas player. In the English Press, in *Wisden*, and in other publications, he was invariably referred to as 'Sussex's South African all-rounder'.

As one born in South Africa, he was, on occasions, subjected to catcalls and insults on grounds up and down the country when individuals of limited mind and no vision sought to hold him responsible for the pernicious doctrines of the South African government of the time. It was a period when emotions ran high on the subject of apartheid. It was a system which Tony Greig condemned unequivocally, just as he feared that it would lead inevitably to a bloodbath.

With a father who was a progressive thinker and who was guided by principles of honour, trust and the dignity and rights of the individual, and with men like Sobers, Kanhai, Lloyd and Gibbs now numbered among his friends, it was unthinkable that Greig should ever be anything else but international in his views. He was not, however, a man who would deny the existence of South Africa or the fact that he was born there. He would not pretend, as some have tried to, that things never happened. He was grateful to South Africa for the education that it had given him, for the sporting opportunities that it had provided and for the friends that he had there whom he loved. He was never willing to deny this part of his heritage, but he felt equally that he was descended from a long line of Scotsmen and that his father had ever kept alive the awareness that the Greigs were British. The concept of dual nationality is perhaps only best understood by those whose parents are of two countries and by those who have lived abroad for any period of time.

Tony Greig returned to England in April 1972, with

excitement bubbling in cricket quarters about his achievements as an all-rounder with the World XI. There was also a faction which stated that he should not play for England because he was a South African. He sought reassurance as to his qualifications, and he was told by the secretary of MCC, Billy Griffith, father of the Sussex captain, that, having played for England against the Rest of the World, 'his bona fides had been established'.

The authorities were to show incredible ambiguity regarding Greig's position over the years. In October 1973, Sussex asked the Registrations Committee to reconsider Greig's status. The Committee again ruled that under the existing regulations Greig was an overseas player. By that time, he had already played for England in nineteen Test matches.

The talk that surrounded Greig at the start of the season made it apparent that the Press, and the selectors, were confident that he would be chosen for the first match of the series against Australia. He needed only to confirm that he was in form to make his selection certain. In a soggy May, this is what he did. He hit 42 and took 3 for 96 against Essex, and 72 not out and took 1 for 23 against Warwickshire. Both matches were ruined by rain. Sussex qualified for the quarter-finals of the first Benson and Hedges Cup, and in the traditional Whitsun match against Middlesex at Lord's, where it always pays to do well, Greig made 3 and 62 and took 1 for 60 as Sussex were trounced. His selection for the First Test was a formality.

In naming Greig, the selectors were creating no precedent. Captains of England like G.O.E.Allen, Freddie Brown, Colin Cowdrey and Ted Dexter had all been born overseas, and the selection of Allen, in particular, caused much adverse comment in the Thirties, for he had been born in Australia.

Greig was the only Test debutant in the England side that took the field at Old Trafford on 8 June 1972.

Illingworth won the toss and England batted. The start was delayed for ninety minutes because of a wet outfield, and Boycott, struck above the left elbow by a ball from Lillee, was forced to retire hurt at lunchtime when he had scored three runs and England had thirteen on the board. Boycott was to resume when the score was 118 for 4, but he made only five more runs.

The weather was cold, the ball moved about appreciably and the going was slow. John Edrich had looked confident, but he ran himself out when one short of his half-century as he attempted to take a short single to Lillee at mid-wicket. This brought Greig in to join D'Oliveira. England's two 'South Africans' were together as, at that time, they could never have been in the country of their birth.

D'Oliveira looked confident, but his first effort brought about his downfall as he played across a ball from Greg Chappell and was bowled. Tony Greig looked nervous and uncertain, but he survived and was still at the crease at the end of the day when, after four hours batting, England had reached 147 for 5. He was something of a nervous starter. Excitable in temperament, he would calm his nerves by smoking before he went out to bat.

On the second morning, in poor light, Greig and Knott stayed together for an hour and a half and extended their partnership to 63. It was a brave and invaluable stand and it took England through the second new ball and through some intricate spin bowling from Gleeson. Knott was out for 18 and Greig was finally leg-before to Colley for 57, the highest score of an England innings which totalled 249.

As John Woodcock was to remark later: 'The England selectors had decided to take a chance with the slip fielding, and it could have easily have cost them the match'. Tony Greig recalled that the day before the game, Ray Illingworth asked for volunteers to field at slip. Greig was a natural choice, for he fielded there on occasions for Sussex and was generally regarded as an outstanding close-to-the-wicket catcher. John Snow also volunteered, and he shaped well in practise. Ray Illingworth completed the slip trio. It was not to be the most lethal of combinations. In his second over, Arnold had Stackpole missed off successive balls by Greig and Snow, and two balls later, Snow put down Francis. Tony also dropped Stackpole off D'Oliveira, but there his anguish ended.

D'Oliveira broke the opening stand when he had Francis leg-before, and 'immediately afterwards when Ian Chappell faced his first ball, England gained their biggest prize'. Greig dropped one a little short and Chappell went for the hook, a shot at which he excelled, only to be caught above his head by Mike Smith who was fielding on the long-leg boundary. This was a wonderful fillip for England, and Greig compounded it when he held the younger Chappell at slip off Snow. The Australian batting fell apart against Snow and Arnold, and England claimed a first innings lead of 147.

By the close of play on Saturday, they were 136 for 3.

The sun shone on the Monday morning and Greig was at the wicket within a few minutes of the start of play. He came in at 140 for 4; when he was out, two and a half hours later, England were 234 for 7, Greig having scored 62 of the runs made while he was at the wicket. It was an innings of panache and its value was emphasized when Lillee took the last three England wickets in four balls so that the last four wickets went down without addition to the score.

Australia, needing 342 to win, were 55 for 2 at the close.

Stackpole and Greg Chappell resumed confidently on the final morning and 55 runs came in the first hour to keep Australia ahead of the clock. Chappell fell to Arnold and Watson to Snow, but the great breakthrough for England came when Greig bowled both Walters and Stackpole. Marsh, who had held five catches in England's second innings, and Gleeson combined in the only three-figure stand of the match. With four hours left, Illingworth turned to Gifford, but Marsh hit him for four mighty sixes.

With the new ball due, Greig returned to the attack. He had Marsh caught behind for 91 with the score on 251, and one run later he bowled Gleeson to give England victory by 89 runs with two and a half hours to spare. Greig's final figures were 4 for 53. It had been a most impressive Test debut and England had won the First Test of a home series against Australia for the first time since 1930.

Australia were to draw level by winning the Second Test, at Lord's, when Massie took 16 wickets. Tony Greig hit England's only half-century of the match.

England were to win at Headingley, and Australia at The Oval so that the series was drawn. Tony Greig scored more runs, 288, at a higher average, 36, than anyone else on the England side, and his ten wickets cost him 39.80 runs each. He also held eight catches.

There was general agreement that England had found the all-rounder for whom they had been searching. E.W.Swanton asserted that England could well be pleased 'with the emergence of Tony Greig as an all-rounder of higher potential than anyone this country has produced for a long time. It looks even clearer now than it did at the time that a young man of such splendid physique and flair should have been chosen to go with MCC to Australia the winter before last.'

Perhaps his non-selection for that tour was a blessing. He had matured much as a cricketer and as a man in the interim, and he broke upon the Test scene in a golden glory. There was such a passionate commitment in all that he did, such an obvious delight

Tony Greig, topped the batting averages for both England and Sussex.

and enjoyment in playing the game that transmitted itself to the spectators and endeared him to them.

He was an automatic choice for the tour of India and Pakistan, but there were still problems with Sussex that had to be faced before he set out on that trip.

In 1972, Sussex were sixteenth in the County Championship, fifteenth in the John Player Sunday League and were beaten in the first round of the Gillette Cup. It was apparent that this annual return of abject results could not be allowed to continue without some effort to reform the state of affairs that existed. Obviously, the county were handicapped in 1972 by the absence of Greig and Snow, for much of the time on Test duty, although Greig had still finished top of the batting averages and shared the bowling honours with his England colleague, but this was no reason for their dreadful season.

On 25 August, close to the end of Sussex's dismal cricketing summer, Mike Griffith announced that he would relinquish the captaincy at the end of the campaign. His resignation came as no surprise, nor, some believed, was it made without some pressure being placed upon him. It would be quite wrong to place all the blame for Sussex's poor record over four or five years squarely on his shoulders, but it was apparent from the outset that he was not the man for the job for reasons which we detailed earlier. His position was never helped by the fact that he had so clearly failed to realize the potential as a player which he had been deemed to possess.

One of the greatest problems that confronted Sussex was the one which had been diagnosed by their president, the Duke of Norfolk. They were an unhappy side, and team-spirit had to be built in the dressing-room.

There were other factors that contributed to Sussex's failure, not the least of which was their policy on overseas players, a policy that was lacking in judgement and foresight.

In 1968, under the new regulations allowing the signing on immediate registration of one overseas player, Sussex engaged Geoff Greenidge. He had eight first-class wickets and 265 runs to his credit for Barbados, and 205 of those runs had come in one innings against Jamaica. It was to be the only double century of his career, and although he played for Sussex until 1975, he averaged under 29 in his 152 matches and ceased to bowl. His record is that of an average, or below-average, county opener. Pleasant man that he was, he could provide nothing for Sussex that would not have been as well or better done by a home-grown player at half the price. Where others had their Procter, Richards, Sobers, Majid Khan or Engineer, Sussex had gone for mediocrity rather than greatness. Their error did not end there.

Their former skipper, the Nawab of Pataudi, recommended that they should engage the Indian all-rounder, Solkar, and he played against the New Zealanders at Hove in 1969. He later returned to India and violated his period of qualification so that he was never seen again for Sussex, who had now turned their attention to another Indian, Udaykumar Joshi.

Joshi was an off-break bowler who was never to play Test cricket. He took 74 wickets for the county in his first season, 1971, after which he declined so that his 33 wickets at more than 40.63 runs each in 1972 represented part of that downward curve. His contract was not renewed after 1974, but by then, as one of Sussex's two permitted specially registered players, he had prevented the county from engaging more talented and more charismatic cricketers, one of whom was Ken McEwan.

McEwan was part of the Queen's College tradition. Tony Greig was impressed by him and, as Mike Buss had done for Greig, so Greig did for McEwan, arranging that he should come on trial to Sussex with a view to signing for them. The presence on the staff of Joshi and Greenidge made this impossible, much to Greig's chagrin, and McEwan was snapped up by Essex. For more than a decade he was to delight crowds up and down the country and he was to play a prominent part in the first successes that Essex were to achieve.

It was vagaries in administration, undistinguished leadership and dissension in the ranks which had brought Sussex to the point of despair. The three were inter-active and the immediate problem was who should try to lead the county out of this trough. They turned to Tony Greig.

Not all were happy with his appointment. 'Criticism was heard,' wrote *Wisden*, 'of Sussex for going outside the county, let alone outside England to find a successor . . .' to Griffith. This hardly seemed fair criticism when one considers that Greig was now an established England cricketer and that past Sussex captains, and great ones, included the Indians, Ranjitsinhji, Duleepsinhji and the Nawab of Pataudi; the South African Alan Melville; and the Australian Murdoch.

Not all were opposed to Greig as captain, of course. As Alan Hill wrote some years later: 'Greig, a devil-may-care madcap with an infectious enthusiasm, was just the tonic Sussex needed to rally their sagging spirits'.

Triumph and Trauma

BEFORE he could give his mind to the job at Sussex, Tony Greig was on his way to India and Pakistan with the MCC side under the captaincy of Tony Lewis, who had not appeared in a Test before the start of the tour. It was an England side that was strong in batting, but not quite so strong in bowling.

Although England won the First Test in India, the Indians took the series by two matches to one, with two drawn. These were the days of the great Indian spin trio, Prasanna, Bedi and Chandrasekhar. They took seventy wickets between them in the five Test matches, whilst the rest of the Indian bowlers managed five.

In Pakistan, all three Test matches were drawn. For Tony Greig, the fourth game was a complete triumph and confirmed his position as an all-rounder of world class. An unbroken fifth-wicket partnership of 101 with Tony Lewis took England to victory over India in the First Test in Delhi. It was England's first win in a Test match in India for 21 years. In the Second Test at Calcutta, Greig took 5 for 24, and England were left to make 192 to win. Greig made 67, but England were bowled out for 163. In the Fifth Test at Bombay, Fletcher and Greig shared a fifth-wicket partnership of 254 which remains an England record for that wicket in all Tests. Greig 'delighted the crowd with the grace and power of his driving and pulling'. He made 148. It was his first Test century.

He topped the England batting averages and scored more runs than any other batsman in the series against India; and he was second in the bowling averages. In the three Tests against Pakistan, he was second to Amiss in the batting and finished behind the spinners, Gifford and Birkenshaw, in the bowling.

Not only was the tour a statistical success for Tony Greig, in India, in particular, he became an immense favourite with the crowds. He was, of course, immediately identifiable, standing over six feet seven inches, blond, commanding, exuding good humour. He was an extrovert cricketer and, if extroverts sometimes upset authority, they are generally the darling of the crowds. The Indians adored Tony Greig and he was at his happiest amongst them. They loved their cricket and they knew that he loved the game as much as they did.

At Eden Gardens, Calcutta, on New Year's Day, 1973, there was the usual banging of drums and clamour from the crowd. On the boundary, Pat Pocock was suddenly pelted with oranges, and there was a fear that the situation would become ugly, but Tony Greig picked up two oranges, pushed them up his jumper and performed an impromptu drag act. The crowd loved it. They loved him, and all ended in laughter and applause.

Greig's enthusiasm and total commitment allied to his excitable temperament had its debit side. In the Third Test in Madras, India had to make only 86 to win. The pitch was turning, but England were without Underwood who had sunstroke. At 11, Engineer, India's leading batsman in the series, was leg-before to Old.

Almost immediately, Ajit Wadekar, the Indian captain, edged Old to Greig at second slip. Greig took the catch knee high and threw the ball in the air in celebration. Wadekar stood his ground. The umpire gave the impression that he was giving Wadekar 'not out'. Greig raced down the wicket with the ball raised high in his hand, a rather threatening sight, while Alan Knott threw a glove in the air and Barry Wood added vocal support. Lewis interposed himself between his players and the umpire, who said that he had been unsighted. He consulted with the square-leg umpire, and Wadekar was given 'out'.

Tony Lewis continues with the postscript to the story. 'I went into the Indian dressing-room and confronted Ajit Wadekar. Shall we play cricket for the next two and a half Tests, or shall we cheat? "Let's play cricket," he said. The whole Indian team nodded but wanted a guarantee that Tony Greig would not continue his acting performance near the bat. I pointed to Abid Ali, Solkar and Engineeer as equal culprits. Solkar was even in the habit of appealing for lbw from the position of short square-leg.'

Donald Carr, the England manager, did not see the incident, but, on reading of it in the Indian Press, he reprimanded Greig and the other England players. On his return to England, Greig was summoned to Lord's and told firmly that gamesmanship and dissent could not be tolerated, however successful the player. Greig felt that it was a temperamental stage of his life and that he was in need of more responsibility. Some felt that he was taking the responsibility before he was offered it. In summing up the series against India in his diary, Tony Lewis felt that it had been the batting that had let his side down and that the presence of Boycott, Edrich and D'Oliveira would have swung the balance in England's favour. He continues: 'As I did my bit for the media, Tony Greig took MCC on a lap of honour. Greiggy has had an adoring audience on this trip. The side were cheered to the heavens and I am proud of them. But what the hell is Greiggy doing out there with my team?'

It should be remembered that this was Greig's first tour with an England side, and that Mike Denness

was England's vice-captain. Yet there was no suggestion that Greig was guilty of using authority. It was
simply the abundance of his enthusiasm and it was
never resented by Denness.

In his appreciation of the tour, Clive Taylor
maintained that Greig and Fletcher were the only two
players who were unqualified successes. Of Greig, he
wrote: 'In every crisis he played with a confidence and
determination that seemed to make big scores
inevitable. As older and more experienced players
shrank in stature before the bowling of Bedi and
Chandrasekhar, so Greig, who initially had as many
problems as any of them, grew. With his catching and
bowling (which is marred only by the indefensibly long
time he takes to get through an over), Greig established
himself as an England player of true all-round ability.
If he can temper his enthusiasm and so curb some
of his mannerisms on the field which are too aggressive
and embarrassing, he will probably go on to become
England's captain.'

These were prophetic words.

Illingworth returned as captain and Boycott was also
available for the home series against New Zealand and
West Indies. It was Tony Greig, however, who
continued to capture the public imagination.

In the First Test against New Zealand, at Trent
Bridge, he took 4 for 33 as the visitors were bowled
out for 97. In England's second innings, he hit a century
off 178 balls in two and a half hours. He went on
to make 139. He showed that 'someone willing to use
his reach and hit the ball could succeed on a pitch
that was not nearly so difficult as everyone imagined'
and 'when he was eventually leg-before to Collinge
he had sixteen fours in possibly the most attractive
innings played for England since the days of Milburn
and Dexter'.

At this time, he was arguably the most popular
cricketer in England. He excelled in the field and always

appeared to be in the game, so that when he dislocated a finger on the first day of the First Test against West Indies at The Oval, England's fielding suddenly seemed slipshod and without vitality. At Lord's, in the Third Test against West Indies — the last of the series— he and Fletcher battled bravely while all about them fell. West Indies made 652 for 8, and all five England bowlers conceded more than a hundred runs; Greig took 3 for 180 in 33 overs. When bowling figures were read out after one spell, and he had conceded more than 150 runs, the crowd roared. Greig lifted both arms as if to accept their acclaim, and the crowd responded with a greater roar and much laughter. His good humour was appriecated, for Tony Greig was one of those rare sportsmen who seemed able to establish a relationship with all who watched him.

In that final Test at Lord's, West Indies crushed England by an innings and 226 runs. It marked the end of Ray Illingworth's term as captain, and Mike Denness was given charge of the side to go to the Caribbean. Denness had taken no part in the Test matches of 1973, but he led England in the Prudential Trophy one-day matches at the end of the season. His appointment was not without its critics, prominent among them being Michael Parkinson who considered the choice 'so barmy one wonders if perhaps they are joking'.

Greig was later to venture that he felt that Denness' appointment was premature, and that he was too inexperienced for the task, albeit he was a successful county captain and a pleasant and intelligent man. Like others, Greig had been shattered by Illingworth's dismissal. He believed Illingworth to be the best tactical skipper he had played under and his tenure of office as captain of England had brought emphatic success until the arrival of Kanhai's side in 1973. There was probably no ulterior motive for dispensing with Illingworth as captain, but there were suspicions, especially in the north, for Brian Close had suffered a similar fate some years earlier.

In the north, too, it was anticipated that Boycott, England's foremost batsman and captain of Yorkshire, would succeed Illingworth. Boycott himself was prepared for the job and wanted it, but he was ever a controversial figure and he was passed over. The slight to Boycott has never been forgotten in many quarters, just as Tony Greig was to remain aware of how precarious is the position of the England captain, how short the memory of selectors, how human their prejudices.

Greig was surprised to find himself named as vice-captain to Denness for the tour of West Indies. He was the man forwarded by the selectors, Alec Bedser, Brian Taylor, Ossie Wheatley and Alan Smith, and the choice met with the wholehearted approval of Mike Denness, who believed Greig to be most capable and to have the full backing of the players.

It was to be a tour of trauma and triumph. There was the initial tension between Boycott and Greig and Denness. Both Greig and Boycott have given their versions. Greig believed that as vice-captain he must support Denness at all times. Boycott felt that he was ever sitting on the fence on important issues. Greig felt that Boycott was not pulling his weight as a senior and influential member of the party. They had a confrontation which initially left their differences unresolved, but they had too much respect for each other for their alienation to last, and, paradoxically, it was their combined efforts which were to help prolong Mike Denness' period of captaincy. Greig and Boycott were to re-emerge in their post-cricketing days as the most entertaining double act in any commentary box.

The First Test, in Port of Spain, Trinidad, was a disaster for England. They were bowled out for 131 on the first day, Greig being the top scorer with 37.

West Indies ended the second day on 274 with Kallicharran and Julien, the seventh-wicket pair, together. Kallicharran had made 142. Denness relates what happened.

'Kallicharran was at the non-striker's end as Derek Underwood bowled the final delivery, which Bernard Julien pushed out on to the off side. Julien then turned to leave the pitch. Kallicharran started to walk down the pitch from the other end when Greig, fielding close in on the off side, hurled the ball at the stumps and hit them. After the last ball was bowled, Bernard Julien, batting at the pavilion end, just did an about turn to walk back to the pavilion. The non-striker, Kallicharran, had to come the full length of the wicket, so by the time the ball was delivered, unless he returned to his crease he was always going to be in play, as it were, until either the ball was dead or the umpire called over and time.

'I was standing at mid-off and as the last ball was played, I saw Tony Greig chase after it. As he threw the ball at the wicket at the non-striker's end, my instinctive reaction was that nobody was backing up at mid-on and if he missed the stumps we were going to give another four runs away. I was actually in the process of setting off to back up myself. As the ball hit the stumps, Kallie was several yards down the wicket, and a bewildered expression came over his face. He just froze. There was an instinctive appeal by Greig and without hesitation the umpire, Douglas Sang Hue, who was moving away from the wicket to get into a correct position, gave Kallicharran out. Kallicharran stood for a few seconds and then walked off, clearly in a tremendous raging temper. He smashed his bat so savagely on the pavilion steps that it broke in two.'

The West Indian crowd reacted in a violently hostile manner. The umpire had not called 'over' and maintained that if he had done, he would not have given the batsman out. Greig had acted instinctively, and he was most upset by the hostility of the West Indian contingent.

Gary Sobers, a great supporter of Greig's, drove him back to the hotel, but Sobers realized that, whatever the rights of the matter, the crowd were unhappy with what they had seen and that, to safeguard the rest of the tour, the batsman should be reinstated.

After a lengthy meeting, it was decided that the solution to the problem was that the appeal should be withdrawn and the batsman reinstated. Nothing that Greig or the England side had done had been against the laws, but the future of the series, it seemed, was at stake. When England arrived at the ground after the rest day they were greeted by angry crowds who seemed prepared for a war of bottle throwing. The reinstatement of Kallicharran avoided that unpleasantness. The West Indies had, during the course of debate, suggested that it might be better for Greig to be flown home.

Not all the England party were happy about the solution, for, according to the laws, Kallicharran was out, and there was gloom and some dissension in the party. Greig discussed the incident with manager Donald Carr and with Mike Denness, and it was accepted that there had been no suggestion of sharp practice, but one wonders in the light of what was to happen a year later whether he was totally forgiven.

Seventeen years later, when West Indies ran out the Australian batsman Dean Jones in controversial circumstances, there was to be no manipulation of the laws and no reinstatement, but then there was no suggestion that the dismissal would cause a riot.

Although Greig, rightly, accepted no blame for what had happened, he began the third day by shaking hands with Kallicharran in the middle of the wicket, a gesture which totally pacified the crowd.

West Indies won the First Test by seven wickets, and the next three Tests were drawn. Greig scored centuries at both Bridgetown and Georgetown in the Third and Fourth Tests.

At Bridgetown, he came to the wicket with England 68 for 4. Fletcher left at 130, and Knott and Greig then added 163, which remains an England sixth-wicket record for the series. Greig went on to take six wickets, including that of Rowe who made 302, for 164 runs as he bore the brunt of the responsibility in the attack. It was the first occasion that a man had scored a century and taken five wickets in the same innings for England. Ian Botham is the only other England cricketer to have achieved the feat.

The final Test was played at Queen's Park Oval, Port of Spain, the same venue at which England had been beaten in the First Test and at which Greig had 'run out' Kallicharran. Denness won the toss, and by the end of the first day, England were 198 for 4, with Boycott 97 not out. He added only two the next morning before being caught behind off Julien, and England were out for 267. Pocock accounted for Fredericks and Kallicharran, but Rowe and Clive Lloyd took West Indies to 174 by the close.

They were still together at lunch on the third day, and the score was 208. Greig had now converted to bowling off-spin.

He was convinced that wickets in West Indies so favoured the batsmen that speed or spin was the only hope of redressing the balance. He had experimented with off-spin bowled around the wicket in the Third Test in Barbados, when he had taken six wickets, and now he tried again. The result was sensational. In the space of twenty balls, he took the wickets of Lloyd, Sobers, Kanhai and Murray at a personal cost of six runs. He soon added the wickets of Julien and Boyce, and Rowe, batting cautiously for his 123, was caught off a full toss to reduce West Indies to 300 for 9. Five runs later, Inshan Ali was leg-before to give Tony Greig figures of 8 for 86. 'In a spell of bowling that will rank among the best in Test history', he took in the day 8 for 33 in 19.1 overs.

England trailed by 38 and had only just cleared those arrears when they lost Amiss. Boycott alone showed the necessary resolution, although he received valuable help from Fletcher and Knott. Boycott hit 112 before being bowled by Gibbs, the ball turning prodigiously, and West Indies needed 226 to win. They ended the fourth day on 30 without loss, and victory seemed a formality. Greig, incidentally, had opened the England attack with his off-spinners.

Of that last day, *Wisden* was to write: 'Perhaps in the end the most decisive factor in the result was the tension that built up during the day. The England players withstood it better than those of West Indies, among whom some of the most experienced seemed to be the most vulnerable.' Greig was to echo this sentiment two years later and was to be castigated for it.

Fredericks and Rowe took their opening stand to 63 before Rowe played back casually to Birkenshaw and was leg-before. Two balls later, Kallicharran was caught at slip, bat and pad, off Greig. Fredericks turned Birkenshaw square on the leg side past Boycott and, amazingly, ran two as the fielder chased the ball. Lloyd was hesitant, and Fredericks, suicidally, was run out by yards. Suddenly, West Indies were 65 for 3.

Greig now took charge and had Kanhai caught at slip, then caught and bowled Lloyd. Sobers, like Kanhai playing in his last Test match, and Murray added 50, but Sobers played over a ball from Underwood and was bowled while Murray drove at Greig and was taken at slip. It was Fletcher's third catch.

Inshan Ali showed a composure which mocked his more experienced teammates, and Boyce bristled with purpose. West Indies were edging closer to victory.

Denness took the new ball after consultation with

Greig, who believed that the bigger seam might aid lift and turn. He was proved right almost immediately as he had Inshan Ali caught by Underwood, and two runs later Geoff Arnold bowled Gibbs to give England a famous victory by 26 runs.

Greig had shown immense stamina and temperamental stability as he sent down 33 overs to take 5 for 70. He was given the honour of leading the side from the field. England had drawn the series. Having been severely criticised, they returned home with honour. The heroes were Greig and Boycott.

Greig's first innings analysis, 8 for 86, and his match analysis, 13 for 156, remain the best by an England bowler against West Indies. He finished second in the England batting averages for the series, scoring nine more runs than Boycott, and top of the bowling averages with 24 wickets.

Had England lost the last Test match, it is likely that Denness would have been replaced as captain, for he had batted with uncertainty throughout the series. Boycott remains convinced that he and Greig re-established Denness' position as England's captain. The axe was about to fall until the victory in Trinidad, Boycott asserts. After it, there were those in authority who did a volte-face.

Boycott was to play in the first Test match of the 1974 series against India and then to undertake a self-imposed exile of three years, thirty Tests, before returning against Australia in 1977.

England won all three Tests against India in 1974 and drew all three against Pakistan. Greig hit a century against India and came close to bringing victory in the First Test against Pakistan. He was unbeaten on 67 with England needing 44 to win with four wickets in hand when rain ended play.

In the autumn, the England party left for Australia. The side was again captained by Mike Denness, but John Edrich, who had not been available for the tour

The England team which met India in the First Test of 1974. Back row (left to right): Keith Fletcher, Chris Old, Bob Willis, Tony Greig, Mike Hendrick, Dennis Amiss. Front row: Derek Underwood, Geoff Boycott, Mike Denness, John Edrich, Alan Knott.

of West Indies the previous winter, was named as vice-captain in place of Tony Greig. The appointment went almost unnoticed, and certainly drew no comment.

Edrich was a senior player, but not a popular or successful captain. If the selectors considered that he must have the job on the grounds of seniority, then why had Boycott not been given the post the previous winter? Denness, who professed a firm support for Greig as his understudy in the Caribbean, now remained silent. Greig was disappointed at being passed over and at being offered neither comment nor explanation. Was the running out of Kallicharran in Trinidad being held against him as a diplomatic misdemeanour? In man-management, those who administer the game have a dreadful record. Tony Greig was to remain ever mindful of this.

The England tour of Australia, 1974-75, was to be one of cricket's great disasters, at least from the point of view of the tourists. It was believed that Dennis Lillee's back injury would have reduced his effectiveness, and of Thomson, little was known except that he had played in one Test against Pakistan two years earlier and had finished with 0 for 110 in 19 overs. By the beginning of December 1974, the names of Lillee and Thomson had become as indissolubly linked in the language of cricket as those of Romeo and Juliet in the field of literature. 'Ashes to Ashes. Dust to Dust. If Thommo don't get you, then Lillee must.'

The pair took thirteen wickets between them in the First Test at Brisbane which Australia won by 166 runs. Australia made 309, and England were reduced to 57 for 4. By the end of the second day, this had increased to 114 for 4 with Edrich 40 and Greig 34. Edrich went early next morning, but Greig found a resolute partner in Underwood and eventually England reached 265. It was a courageous fight-back, and it was due almost entirely to Tony Greig, who made 110 before being caught behind off Lillee. It was the first century by an England batsman in a Test match at Brisbane since Leyland's hundred in 1936-37. It was, according to John Thicknesse, 'a memorable mixture of brilliant off-side strokes, wild passes, and continual attempts to rattle Lillee by shadow-boxing underneath the bouncers'. He batted for five hours and hit fifteen fours.

Not only did England lose the Test match by 166 runs, they also lost Amiss, who had done so well in the West Indies, with a broken thumb, and Edrich with a broken hand. Colin Cowdrey was flown out from England as an emergency replacement. It was his sixth tour of Australia, but nobly as he tried, he could not prevent Australia from winning the Second Test by nine wickets. Greig, now promoted to number four in the England side, hit 23 and 32.

Back at number six, he hit 60 in the second innings of the Third Test which was drawn in an exciting manner. Australia needed only 55 to win from the last fifteen eight-ball overs with four wickets standing. They seemed to have lost their way, and Denness took the new ball, only to see Marsh launch a violent attack which made an Australian victory seemingly certain. Greig dismissed Marsh, but Walker and Lillee maintained the necessary scoring rate. The thirteenth over arrived with only 16 needed, but Greig bowled a splendid over from which only two runs were scored. Underwood followed this with a maiden, and Greig dismissed Lillee with the fourth ball of the last over. Australia finished eight runs short of victory.

Denness dropped himself from the Fourth Test, and Edrich led the side. He returned for the Fifth, and in the Sixth, the last, he hit 188 and England won by an innings. Fletcher also hit a century, and Greig made 89 as well as taking 4 for 88 in Australia's second innings. It must be added that Australia were without Thomson in this match.

In the First Test against New Zealand in Auckland, Tony Greig hit 51, had match figures of 10 for 149, and England again won by an innings, but the match was overshadowed by the injury to Chatfield, who was hit by a bumper from Peter Lever and came close to death.

Denness hit 181, and Fletcher 216, in this match, but there were already suggestions that, at Test level, Denness had been found wanting both as a batsman and as a captain. Certainly, as a batsman, he was incapable of coping with the pace of Lillee and Thomson.

There were times when his captaincy appeared to have been usurped as others made alterations in the field, but, in truth, the Australians, superb in the field,

Tony Greig, caught at slip off Jeff Thomson in the First Test at Sydney during the 1974-5 Ashes series.

would have been too good for any side that England might have fielded at that time. Only two men played the Australian pace attack with consistent confidence and resolution, and those two were Alan Knott and Tony Greig, the only two to play in all six Tests.

'Nothing paints a clearer picture of the overthrow of England's main batting,' wrote John Thicknesse, 'than that of Greig and Knott, who batted mainly at numbers six and seven, were responsible for eight of the fourteen scores of fifty and above. They stood out as the successes of the tour, while Greig's flamboyance gave the side character in the field.'

Indeed, they were the successes. Greig scored more runs than anyone else on the England side, and his seventeen wickets placed him on a par with Willis and Underwood. Moreover, he seemed the one person in the England side capable of giving as good as he got from the Australians.

John Woodcock, in his résumé of the tour, considered that 'Greig nailed down his reputation as an incorrigible cricketer whose relationship with the Australian public, and their players too, was tempestuous'. His personality dominated the series. Beautiful girls in bikinis would invade the ground to claim a kiss, and Greig maintained a love-hate relationship with the Australian spectators which Bryon Butler, in *The Cricketer*, analysed clearly and prophetically. 'The reason, probably, is that they recognize in this man a kindred soul. A competitor of his type, they doubtless reason, should be playing for Australia and not for the Pommies.'

There was an exuberance, an unashamed delight, in Greig's cricket which the Australians appreciated, but which was something new to the English. There had been joyful cricketers, Compton and Edrich amongst them, but none quite so manifestly extrovert as Tony Greig. At a time when England were being walloped, it was heartening, and it caught the imagination of both Press and public.

The only real crime that Mike Denness committed, like David Gower after him, was to captain an England side against a team that was too strong for them. Like Douglas in 1921, he was also to have his misdemeanour compounded in that his opponents followed him back to England from Australia, but before he could cope with them he had to negotiate the inaugural World Cup, which was sponsored by Prudential.

England's path to the semi-finals was very smooth. The opening game of the competition produced one of the most dreadful of one-day games. Amiss scored 137, England hit 334 for 3, and India made 132 for 3 in their allotted 60 overs. Gavaskar batted throughout that time for 32.

New Zealand were beaten by 80 runs in the second match, Fletcher making 131 and Greig taking four wickets, which left only the formality of victory over East Africa.

The semi-final against Australia at Headingley turned out to be a controversial affair in that the strip had already been used only two days earlier and provided the bowlers with a dream surface. England were bowled out for 93 in 36.2 overs, and Australia lost six wickets in passing that total.

Australia lost a magnificent World Cup Final to West Indies and remained in England to play four Test matches which had not been in the original calendar.

The First Test, at Edgbaston in July, was the final disaster for Mike Denness. He won the toss and asked Australia to bat first. It was unlikely that he took this decision without discussing it with the selectors first, yet an article by Jim Laker in the *Daily Express* stated that a selector was absolutely shattered when he heard that England had put Australia in to bat.

In electing to field, Denness ran the risk of his batsmen facing the formidable Australian attack on

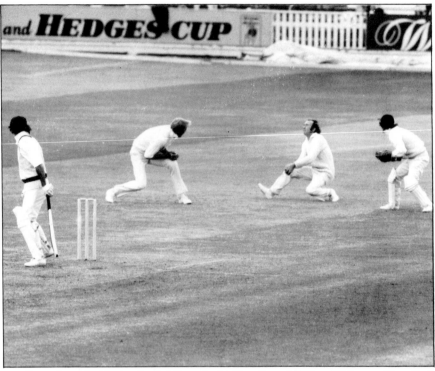

Ian Chappell caught Fletcher bowled Snow in the First Test of 1975 at Edgbaston. Tony Greig is at second slip.

a wet wicket. This is just what happened. Denness was also criticised for under-using Derek Underwood. Gooch, making his Test debut, was twice dismissed for nought; Denness made 3 and 8; and England were crushed by an innings.

Denness was later to write that, on reading Laker's newspaper article on the second morning of the Test, he determined to resign as England captain. The Sword of Damocles had long been hanging over him, and it came as no surprise to the general public to learn that he was to be replaced as England captain.

The public was also not surprised to learn that his successor was to be Tony Greig.

Tony Greig looks on as Rick McCosker is bowled by Geoff Arnold.

This time Tony raises his arms in triumph as Greg Chappell is given out lbw to Chris Old.

109

Delight for England. Max Walker is bowled by John Snow at Edgbaston. Chris Old and Tony Greig are the delighted fielders.

Opposite page: Tony Greig caught Marsh bowled Walker on a rain-affected Edgbaston wicket.

Captain
of England

TONY Greig says that he had no idea how close he was to the England captaincy until he read the Sunday newspapers during the rest day of the First Test at Edgbaston, yet his appointment cannot have come to him as a great surprise. Denness' position had been in question from the start when he was named as captain for only the first of the four Tests against Australia, and the Sunday Press, almost without exception, crucified him after the third day of that Test.

Greig had much sympathy for Denness in the way that he was treated by the Press and reflects that he resolved that if he were to become captain of England, he 'would never slide into the position in which Mike Denness was now languishing. I would get out before I could be crucified.'

He remembers how he sat in a Birmingham pub and considered the England captains that he had known: 'Ray Illingworth, who had won, then retained the Ashes, oddly sacked after one poor series; Tony Lewis, who had done a splendid, if defeated job with an understrength side in India, dismissed and scarcely heard of again as a player. There seemed little doubt that the England job was an unpredictable one in which you needed both a share of luck and a good side to survive.'

A telephone call from Alec Bedser told Greig of his appointment, and Greig, in turn, phoned Mike Denness and offered his condolences, a gesture that was much appreciated.

Tony Greig had been captain of Sussex since 1973,

and he led the side until the end of the 1977 season. The county's record was far from spectacular during those years. There was a much better record in the John Player League and a place in the Gillette Cup Final in his first season as captain, but it was generally a moderate record. Tony Greig maintains that his main object as captain of Sussex was to remain unfulfilled because the county won nothing under his leadership, but his achievements could not be measured in terms of victories and defeats. He made Sussex a happier club and a better place in which to play cricket.

There was much to be put right behind the scenes in the administration and in the encouragement of young players, and he did much to bring these things about. The staff become stronger, more ambitious and far happier. He was, in Alan Hill's words, a 'combative, exciting and inspirational cricketer', and he infected people with his enthusiasm. He was, too, by 1975, when he became captain of England, at the peak of his powers. The season was to bring him 56 wickets and 1,699 runs, including five centuries, one of which was the only double century of his career.

Against Warwickshire, at Hastings, on the last day of May, he came to the wicket with Sussex at 24 for 3. 'The true greatness of Greig, the Sussex captain, was seen in this match,' wrote *Wisden*. In four and a quarter hours, he hit 226 which included six sixes and eighteen fours. He shared stands of 191 with Parsons, and of 147 with Snow. His innings ended when, having hit the first four balls of a Lewington over for sixes, he was caught at long-on by Amiss off the fifth.

His approach to captaincy, like his approach to cricket in general, was enthusiastic, wholehearted, energetic and uncompromising. Sussex finished bottom of the County Championship, but no blame was attached to Greig and more people came to watch them. However limited and unbalanced the side, they were improving and exciting, and all could see it. It was no surprise when they climbed to tenth the following season.

In reviewing the 1975 season, Jack Aldridge could find nothing but praise for Greig in all that he did: 'When Greig was appointed England's captain in July, the tall South African handled the ensuing Press, radio and television interviews with great assurance, and relish. He was no less confident when asked to join the BBC panel of cricket commentators and was certainly shouldering the burden of leading England, as well as his county eleven, a dauntless task for any man, with tremendous spirit and drive. These qualities had been displayed in no uncertain manner at Hastings against Warwickshire, with a dazzling double century in the Championship match, and a powerfully-struck hundred in the John Player League fixture. Greig's determination was also to the fore when he issued a tersely-worded statement deploring the too-cautious batting tactics of the Australians at Hove.'

If being appointed captain of England came as a surprise to Tony Greig, it came as a surprise to few others. He was the people's choice.

Some four months before he was named as England's captain, *The Cricketer* had featured an article by Paul Weaver which was entitled *Greig — cricket's greatest personality.* 'Greig succeeds,' wrote Weaver, 'because he leaves any fear of self-doubt behind him when he steps on the cricket field. He is always positive and attacking. As a future England captain his boldness and lack of discretion may be viewed as more of a disadvantage. As captain of Sussex since September 1972 he has been, at times, impatient with some of his young, inexperienced and not a little frightened players. But time will surely give him understanding, and the ability to handle players according to their individual needs.'

By the start of the season, it was Greig rather than

Denness or Edrich, who was being asked for his views on cricket matters by the BBC and as a member of a panel convened by the Lord's Taverners. There was general relief and universal rejoicing when he was named as captain of England.

In the first place, he had already become only the third England player to have scored 2,000 runs and to have taken 100 wickets in Test cricket. In this feat, he had emulated Wilfred Rhodes and Trevor Bailey.

In the second place, his aggression seemed to deny failure. His dynamism was the infusion that England needed. It did not guarantee instant success, but, as at Sussex, it would make life happier and more eventful. Third, his appointment brought to an end the political intrigue, bickering and character assassination that had marked the end of Denness' tenure of office.

Greig was, as Tony Lewis said at the time of his appointment as captain of England, 'of the breed who appear successful even when they are failing. He will roll one arm then the other as he walks to bat, looking as if he is prepared to strike the ball hard even if he is in poor form. He will twist his off-spin or thump in a seamer, and transfix the batsman with a wide-eyed mixture of threat and astonishment even though the ball has been met with the middle of the bat.' He was an encouraging sight. He lightened hearts. He gave hope. He beckoned others to follow his path. The beginning of his career as captain of England had more than a tinge of romance about it, but then so had so much of his life.

The side that Greig helped to choose for the Lord's Test showed four changes from the team that had lost at Edgbaston. Barry Wood, David Steele, Bob Woolmer and Peter Lever replaced Mike Denness, Keith Fletcher, Chris Old and Geoff Arnold. The selection that took all by surprise was that of David Steele. He was thirty-three years old, had been a Northamptonshire player for twelve years and was a rugged and determined, rather than stylish batsman. Greig knew him as a fighter and as a man who longed to play for England. He realized, too, that Steele was a man who would give him unflinching loyalty. His selection was an inspiration, and David Steele, with his grey hair, rimless glasses, hunched walk and infectious good-humour, became a national celebrity over-night.

Greig always possessed a wonderful sense of the dramatic, of what was good theatre. He came down the steps of the Lord's pavilion and strode to the middle to toss with Ian Chappell. He indicated nothing, but turned to walk a few paces back to the pavilion before swinging round to gesture to the groundstaff at the Nursery End that he wanted the heavy roller. England had won the toss.

Thomson was erratic and constantly over-stepped the mark; Lillee was lethal. He trapped Wood, Amiss and Edrich leg-before and had Gooch taken behind. Tony Greig entered in the familiar situation of England at 49 for 4. He had placed his faith in Steele, and he was rewarded as the Northamptonshire batsman helped him to add 96 before dragging a ball from Thomson on to his stumps as soon as he had reached fifty.

Tony Greig shared a stand of 77 with his old warrior ally Alan Knott. Then, only four short of his century, he edged Walker to Ian Chappell at slip. He had taken the attack to the enemy. His 96 had come in 160 minutes and included fifteen fours. This was heroism spiced with panache, and the capacity crowd loved it. In one afternoon, he had stamped his personality on the England captaincy. Whatever the responsibilities of the job, they would not impair his ability.

England were all out on the second morning for 315. By lunch, they were in total command. Snow, who had wrongly been omitted from the party which toured Australia, bowled an inspired spell. Peter Lever gave admirable support and Australia were 64 for 6. Greig recalls that the reception the side received as they left the field and entered the Long Room was one of the most memorable of his career. England's pride had been regained.

Australia recovered from the despair of 81 for 7 through an excellent 99 from Ross Edwards and a swashbuckling 73 not out from Dennis Lillee, and England's lead was only 47. There followed a mighty 175 from John Edrich, the first streaker at Lord's — Michael Angelow, a merchant seaman, who hurdled over both sets of stumps and was arrested and fined £20 — and rain after Greig had set Australia the task of scoring 484 in 500 minutes. It was all something of an anticlimax.

Greig's appointment had been in response to popular demand, and he had not let his public down. His philosophy was clear. 'I want blokes who are prepared to go out there and die on the field. Guts and determination are so important.' They were not qualities in which Greig himself was lacking.

For the Third Test, at Headingley, Greig caused another surprise by bringing in another man not lacking in the qualities he insisted upon, Phil Edmonds. The Middlesex left-arm spinner responded by producing a spell of 5 for 17 from the pavilion end in his first twelve overs in Test cricket. This helped to tumble Australia out for 135, and England led by 153. Eventually, Australia were left with the task of making 445 to win. They ended the fourth day on 220 for 3 so the game was beautifully balanced, the odds slightly in England's favour. Alas, there was to be no play on the last day.

When the players awoke it was discovered that the pitch had been vandalized during the night by a group who were attempting to draw attention to the innocence of one George Davis, who had been imprisoned for a crime in East London. Davis' name had long been daubed on bridges and walls along the Commerical Road, now his champions sought a larger audience.

Davis was later freed, but he was quickly rearrested when he was involved in another crime.

The Fourth Test at The Oval was alloted six days and was the longest to be played in this country. England were forced to follow-on, but they made 538 in their second innings, their highest second-innings total against Australia, and the match was drawn. Greig had brought England back to a position of equality with Australia, mentally if not statistically, by drawing the last three Tests. This was a good achievement and Greig was rightly proud of what he had accomplished, but he was also conscious of, and upset by, criticisms that England had not won.

There was no tour that following winter, and he spent the time in Australia, playing grade cricket for Waverley in Sydney and engaging in business affairs. In the light of what was to happen later, this was an important winter for him.

He travelled extensively in Australia and developed several business contacts. He was a much sought-after personality and he became heavily involved in publicity and public relations, being asked to endorse a variety of products. He was the man of the moment, and it is necessary to grasp such a moment, for the life of a cricketer and of a celebrity can be very short indeed.

More significantly for Tony Greig, he was asked to become a member of the commentary team for the television coverage of the series between Australia and West Indies which Australia were to win most emphatically. It was during this series that he began to develop commentary techniques which stirred emotions when he later joined Channel Nine and Sky Television. Wes Hall and Bill Lawry were part of the commentary team and Greig was excited to see how they could be played off, one against the other, bringing the viewer closer to the game as they relived past experiences and, through those experiences, gave a sharper definition of what was happening in the current match.

His involvement with television commentating and journalism did not prevent Greig from enjoying his cricket with Waverley in Sydney. He led the club to their first Premiership for 31 years, scoring 544 runs at an average of 32 and taking 75 wickets at 12.3 runs each. This was the greatest number of wickets that anyone had taken in the competition since Bill O'Reilly's 147 in 1943-44. Unfortunately, the grand Final of the Premiership in 1975-76, between Waverley and Bankstown-Canterbury, was completely washed out, but Tony Greig had again made his mark in Australia. He had also learned much about England's opponents in the summer of 1976, West Indies, and, on 18 May, it was announced that he had been appointed England's captain for all five Tests.

He had studied the techniques and methods of the West Indian side in Australia and drew up a plan of campaign with which he would oppose them in England. West Indies had lost five Tests to one in Australia, but no one doubted that they were an outstanding side. In Michael Holding, they had a bowler whom Greig considered to be the fastest he ever faced, and he was most ably supported by two other very quick and very fine bowlers, Andy Roberts and Wayne Daniel. Their batting revolved around Clive Lloyd, Gordon Greenidge and the rising star of Viv Richards, who was to complete a thousand Test runs in a calendar year. Well beaten as they had been in Australia, they had still scored their runs at an astonishing 4.66 per eight-ball over throughout the series. Where they had failed was in the temperamental instability that they had shown. Holding was one who had displayed lapses of discipline and he was to continue to show such lapses in the next few years. This was seen by many to be the area in which the West Indians were most vulnerable.

Greig argued that with the limited fire-power at his disposal, he would adopt a defensive attitude in the field against West Indies and would concentrate on frustrating them so evoking those weaknesses in temperament which had been their downfall in Australia. It was a method which had its parallels in the way in which Greig himself had confronted Lillee and Thomson.

There was nothing particularly novel in Greig's line of thinking. He was, in effect, giving recognition to an Achilles' heel which, as we have said, many believe existed. In an interview before the series he spoke of the strength of West Indies, but, following the common line of argument, he stated that when things went wrong for them, West Indies tended to fall apart. He said that it was his intention that England 'would make the West Indies grovel'.

It seemed at the time an innocent remark, a vivid piece of imagery, an example of 'what oft was thought, but ne'er so well expressed', but it was to prove an unhappy remark for Greig.

'I was chased around the country that summer by the acrimony my "grovel" remark had stirred up.' He believed it had been a mistake, but it did not dissuade him from the belief that cricket needed men who would offer their opinion honestly and uncompromisingly.

Mike Brearley, a firm supporter of Greig, considered that the remark would have been tactless from any source, 'but in the mouth of a blond South African it carried an especially tasteless and derogatory tone'. That was always Greig's problem. When all was going well, he was England's captain, a great all-rounder. When there were crises from which others might wish to become disassociated, he was again a tall, blond South African.

His defensive policy did not work in the First Test against West Indies at Trent Bridge, but the game was drawn. Viv Richards hit 232 out of West Indies' 494, but, thanks to a century from David Steele, England made 332 in reply. Needing 339 to win in 315 minutes, England ended on 156 for 2. Greig was criticized for delaying the introduction of Underwood into the attack on the first day. The Kent left-arm spinner later accounted for Richards, Lloyd, Kallicharran and Gomes, an impressive haul. The success of David Steele, however, was a credit to Greig.

He had always believed qualities of character to be the most important reason for selecting a player, and 'the brilliant selection', as Brearley was to call it, of Steele was conceived by Greig. Brearley himself was a Greig selection for the First Test and it was Greig who insisted upon the recall of Brian Close, another tough fighter.

The chairman of the selection committee was to have the casting vote from 1977 onwards if there was any deadlock over the choice of a player, but in 1976, the casting vote was held by the captain, and Greig used it to have Close in his side. Hutton, one of the selectors, had been absent from the meeting, and his tenure of office was to be short, but it is unlikely that Greig would have had his way had Hutton been present. Hutton did not approve of Greig's positive approach. He believed him 'a little too sure of himself for my comfort', and he also found Greig too outspoken. Following the 'grovel' remark, Hutton advised Greig as the team was setting out for India not to say too much.

The selection battle that Greig did lose was that regarding Geoff Boycott. He wanted Boycott for the series, but Boycott was injured for nine weeks. He was also certain that he could persuade his fellow selectors to name Boycott as vice-captain for the tour to India, 1976-77, an appointment which would have led to Boycott fulfilling his ambition of becoming captain of England in due course. Boycott 'respected the fact that Greig had bent over backwards for me at our

121

Lord's in 1976. Tony Greig looks on as the Queen meets veteran Yorkshire cricketer Brian Close.

meeting earlier in the season and I knew I could play happily under him', but there were divisions among the selectors and Boycott's return to Test cricket was not to be brought about until 1977, by which time Brearley was captain of England. The part played by Tony Greig in achieving this should not be under-estimated, however, for Boycott played for Waverley in Sydney in the 1976-77 season, and he and Greig discussed matters there before the England team went to India.

The Second Test at Lord's in the scorching summer of 1976 began badly for England. Greig won the toss, but his side batted with such caution that they ended the first day on 197 for 8 from 80.4 overs. This was supplemented by some bold hitting from Old and Underwood on the second morning, and England reached 250. Greig quickly brought Underwood into the attack when West Indies batted, and the Kent man rewarded him by taking five wickets. The England fielding was brilliant and the sounds of *Rule Britannia* emanated from the old Tavern area as the visitors were bowled out for 182.

There was no play on the Saturday, and eventually West Indies faced a target of 323 in approximately five hours. Fredericks led the charge for victory with an innings of 138, which ended when he was caught at deep mid-off. In the next over, Lloyd was bowled by Greig, and as he returned to the pavilion, the West Indies captain indicated that he was satisfied to settle for a draw, but Greig insisted on continuing. He crowded the bat with close fielders, and Underwood bowled Gomes and Julien. Only when three balls remained and four wickets still stood would Greig leave the field.

The teams went to Old Trafford for the Third Test with the series still level. For England, and for Greig, this was to be an unhappy match. Mike Selvey was given his Test baptism and took four wickets as West

Indies were bowled out for 211. He also took two wickets in the second innings which ended only when Lloyd declared on 411 for 5. England made 71 and 126. *Wisden* was to describe the pitch on which England batted as 'cracked, often unpredictable'. Greig was more forceful. He believes the pitch to have been the most dangerous and unpredictable on which he ever played a Test, and a year later he wrote to that effect, stating that Old Trafford should not stage a Test match if the Lancashire club could not produce better. He was fined by the TCCB for this truth. Mike Brearley supported his view.

Greig had been concerned about the quality of the wickets at Hove, but some forceful talking to groundsman Peter Eaton had brought about an improvement. His criticism of the Old Trafford pitch was coupled with the fact that England were confronted by Daniel, Holding and Roberts, and that Holding was lucky to be the only one to be warned for intimidatory bowling. Greig was scathing in his criticism of the Lancashire groundsman and the authorities for producing such conditions. Of the West Indies bowlers and of Edrich and Close, he said, 'Two of the bravest English batsmen of my time were reduced to wrecks by a short-pitched assault unparalleled in its danger during my experience'. This was the low point of Tony Greig's cricket career.

The chairman of selectors, Alec Bedser, with whom Greig had a surprisingly good relationship, made a point of giving the England captain a public vote of confidence during the Old Trafford Test, but such announcements, as football managers know to their cost, are usually the prelude to dismissal. Greig's batting average after three Tests was 7.6, and he felt that the fast men had finally conquered him. His worries about the Old Trafford wicket had caused him to be more concerned with the protection of his life than of his wicket. He believed that he failed as a captain in tactics and in example, and he was on the point of resignation. Alan Knott, always a faithful ally, persuaded him otherwise. The real Greig reasserted himself and fought back.

He had long adopted the raised-bat style in dealing with the fast bowlers. If one stands over six feet seven inches, it is a style almost imposed upon one. Brearley and others were to imitate it, and it has come in for much criticism, but for Greig, it was highly effective. He watched video recordings of his innings against West Indies and was severe in his self-criticism. He saw that in his eagerness not to be dominated by the bowling, he was over-anxious to attack and that he was trying to hit the ball too hard with the full swing of the bat rather like the average tennis player who, when faced by a hard service, is drawn into trying to return the ball twice as hard.

He took his brother, Ian, then seventeen, to the nets and Ian, bowling briskly off some seventeen yards, provided unrelenting practise which included a fair sprinkling of short pitched deliveries.

England lost by 55 runs at Headingley in the Fourth Test and so lost the series, but they won back their self-respect. Greig's contribution was monumental. West Indies, with Fredericks and Greenidge putting on 192 for the first wicket, reached 330 for 2, but England clawed their way back and dismissed the visitors for 450. In reply, they slumped to 80 for 4. Balderstone helped Greig in a partnership of 89, and Greig and Knott then added 152. Both batsmen scored 116, and England finished only 63 behind on the first innings. Had either of them failed, England would have been doomed.

Inspired by Bob Willis, one of five changes to the side which had taken the field at Old Trafford, England bowled out West Indies for 196 in their second innings, so were left to score 260 to win. The hopes of victory seemed dashed in Roberts' first four overs when, bowling at a furious pace and maintaining an unwavering line of attack, the fast bowler sent back Steele, Hayes and Balderstone as England reached 23. Willey stood firm and he and Woolmer added 57 before Woolmer fell leg-before to Holder. Greig and Willey then carried the fight to the West Indies. In fifty thrilling minutes on the fourth evening, they added 60 runs, and an epic victory looked possible. Shortly before the close, Willey flicked Holding to square-leg where Roberts took a fine diving catch.

In his first twenty-three deliveries the next morning, Daniel took the wickets of Underwood, Knott and Snow while Greig stood frustrated, pinned down by three successive maidens, at the bowler's end. With only Ward and Willis now left to help him, Greig threw his bat and 46 runs were added. England were 56 runs short of victory when Holding accounted for Ward and Willis with successive deliveries. Greig remained unbeaten on 76. 'His attempt to win the match off his own bat,' wrote John Woodcock, 'when only Ward and Willis were left to help him, was larger than life.'

In the Fifth Test at The Oval, Richards hit 291, Amiss 203 and Holding took 14 for 149 on a batsman's pitch. West Indies won by 231 runs. A week later, Greig was named as captain of the England side to tour India in the early months of 1977 with Mike Brearley as his vice-captain. It would have been difficult for the selectors to have chosen Brearley to lead the side as his Test debut had come only in the first match of the series against West Indies, and he had been dropped after the Second Test.

It was probably this fact alone that saved Greig. No man had a sterner initiation as captain of England. His first eight Tests had been against the world's fastest bowlers, and he had been asked to fight them with amunition which, if not dud, was far from lethal. Few considered these facts when severe criticisms were levelled at Greig and at his captaincy.

Between them Alan Knott and Tony Greig fail to catch the West Indies' Roy Fredericks in the last Test at The Oval in 1976.

Shortly after his appointment as captain for the tour of India, he was interviewed by the BBC and asked his response to the criticisms that had been made of his handling of the England side. He reflected that he was troubled by the criticisms of those who had been leading players, but that he realized that such criticism was an integral part of the job of being captain of England, especially when the side was being beaten. He knew, but did not say, that there were those who would liked to have had him replaced by Brearley, and for a variety of reasons, social and geographical. He was too intelligent a man not to realize that being captain of England was a tenuous office and that one could be replaced by the whim or the political persuasion of one in authority.

127

In *The Cricketer*, H.F.Ellis talked of his captaincy in the one-day international match at Lord's when Barlow, Gooch and Randall all went to the wicket before Greig as England slumped to 31 for 3 as not just bad captaincy, but 'non-captaincy carried out to the ultimate degree'. Six months later, Tony Greig was to be re-established as a hero.

Assessing himself as a captain, Greig was to say that he never considered himself to be a great leader when it came to strategy, and that his main qualities of captaincy had always been his ability to motivate players, to make them want to win. In terms of strategy, he would consult with his senior players in the England side, and they would pool their resources. That is true, but he was never afraid to assert command when he thought it necessary, and he thought about the game deeply.

He won his first battle as soon as his side arrived in India. At the initial Press conference, he told the Indian journalists that their country possessed some of the best umpires in the world and that he was not prepared to condemn them because of any outbursts on the part of previous touring captains. It was a stroke of diplomatic genius, and it paved the way for a successful tour.

He had been planning for this series since he had visited India with Tony Lewis' team in 1972-73. He responded to the vast crowds in India, and they adored him. In Mike Brearley's words, 'Greig understood pageantry'. There are not many in cricket in recent years who are able to say the same. Before each Test on the 1977 tour, the England side would parade in their blazers, trimmed with orange and yellow, and salute each section of the crowd. It is a gesture which links player and spectator and it has been adopted since by leading soccer clubs. After the Second Test, in Calcutta, the England side did a lap of honour and the Indian crowd cheered and clapped in spite of the fact that their team had just been beaten by ten wickets.

Greig always understood the need to bring closer together those who were paid for playing the game and those who paid to come through the turnstiles to watch them. It is an indictment of many who run the game today that they have failed to follow his example and can even be accused of treating the paying customer with contempt.

His response to the crowd, his feeling for pageantry, never allowed Greig to be swayed from the seriousness of his mission. He was, like Close and Illingworth before him, tough, but considerate. He was a disciplinarian, but he had compassion. His experience of India had told him that the leading Indian batsmen were fine players of spin, and therefore he decided that England would attack tham with the faster bowling of John Lever, Bob Willis and Chris Old. The spin of Derek Underwood would be used primarily as a defensive weapon, although, as it transpired, this defence was to be a potent form of attack. The policy was to work magnificently.

Greig had set a precedent as a captain in that he had led his side on to the field at something of a trot. His emphasis was on urgency of a job to be done. If Brearley found him at times prone to swing too violently between the polarities of defence and attack, he formed the highest admiration and respect for Greig. He recognized that he possessed that intuitive quality with which only the best of captains is endowed. He knew when to interfere, when to stand back. He knew the very moment at which it was necessary to intervene in any situation. He had, too, the ability to get the best out of men because he could identify with all of them. He understood those who wished to socialize and those who wished to lead a quiet life, and he could reconcile both views. His sensitivity to people was something, perhaps, which was not readily perceived by those who saw only the showman exterior.

In the First Test, in Delhi, shortly before Christmas 1976, Brearley was run out as England started disastrously, losing their first four wickets for 65 runs. A week later, Greig told Brearley that he could have cried for him when he was run out. Brearley was deeply touched, particularly as he believed that Greig was a captain who rarely watched the cricket when his side was batting. Brearley was to learn much from Greig on this tour which was to refine his own highly intelligent and personal views on captaincy.

A mammoth innings of 179 by Dennis Amiss and some masterly bowling by John Lever, who took 7 for 46 in India's first innings and 3 for 24 in the second on the occasion of what was his Test debut, set up England's first innings victory in India. Having scored 381, England bowled out India for 122 and 234. Lever was later accused by Bedi, the Indian captain, of having greased the ball in some manner, but the accusation was dismissed with tact and humour by Greig and the bowler, and the series proceeded peacefully.

The captain knew when to assert himself and he reset Underwood's field in the second innings when a couple of boundaries had been hit, sending people deeper. Underwood was not a bowler who enjoyed captains meddling with his field, but Greig had felt that the situation was becoming rudderless and that there was need for authority. Underwood finished with 4 for 78.

From the start of the tour, Greig had emphasized to his pace men that there was a necessity to bowl flat out at the Indian tail-enders, to make them feel uncomfortable at the crease so that no cheap runs were given away because bowlers were coasting and not giving sufficient energy to the job of removing the last two or three wickets. They heeded his words, for Bedi, Prasanna and Chandrasekhar scored only 156 runs between them in 28 innings during the series.

If Greig's pounding of his bowlers that they must

Indian spectators express their feelings over the 'Vaseline incident'.

be unrelenting in their attitude towards tail-enders seemed stern, it was as nothing compared to what happened on the evening of Christmas Day. He was delighted at the victory in Delhi, but he feared a repetition of the fate that had befallen Lewis' side when resounding victory in the First Test had been followed by two defeats and the loss of the series. He felt that this was due, in part, to complacency, and he saw the same thing happening again. The innings win in Delhi and the seasonal festivities had combined to suggest a relaxation in attitudes. Keith Fletcher had fallen, accidentally, at a party on Christmas Eve and sustained an ankle injury which was to keep him out of the next two Tests. No one was to blame, but to Greig it seemed symptomatic of the dangerous laxity that was creeping over the side. He called a team meeting for six o'clock on Christmas Day.

The players believed it was to be another social gathering. Some arrived late, one failed to arrive at all. Greig gave them a verbal castigation the like of which they had heard from no captain before. He told them forcibly that the purpose of the tour was to win the Test series and that over-rode all other considerations. He walked out, leaving them in stunned silence as he slammed the door for dramatic effect. It was uncharacteristic of the man, but it was a calculated move which he felt was necessary. Ken Barrington, the tour manager, found him sipping a cup of coffee and remarked that he had heard some strong talks, but never one like that which Greig had just delivered. Greig knew that he ran the risk of inciting a resentment among the players because of the strength of his tirade, but he believed that his faith in their dedication as professionals and in their loyalty to him would avert this. He was proved to be right. He always had the additional power that he led by example.

The Second Test began in Calcutta on New Year's Day, 1977. On 6 January, England won by ten wickets. It was a victory achieved by resolute batting, accurate bowling and brilliant fielding. It was the first time England had ever won in Calcutta, and it was the first time that England had won two successive Tests in India. England's inspiration came from their own dedication and from the performance of their captain.

All grass had been removed from the pitch on New Year's Eve, and when Bedi won the toss it seemed that India had gained an immense advantage. Willis, Lever, Underwood and Old bowled such an admirable line, that India lost seven wickets in scoring a meagre 147 on the opening day. The determination and unity of the England side is something that Greig recalls with pride and pleasure. They bubbled in the hotel in the evening, and on the second morning Willis and Old quickly disposed of the last three batsmen. India were all out for 155.

Amiss and Barlow began the England innings, but Barlow soon fell to Madan Lal. When Bedi brought himself into the attack the crowd erupted, and the great left-arm spinner had Brearley taken at short-leg before the conclusion of his first over. Randall and Amiss both passed 30 before falling to Prasanna, and Greig joined Tolchard, who was making his Test debut in place of the injured Fletcher, with the score on 90 for 4.

Tony Greig has said since that his one thought was to survive the final session so that he would be at the wicket on the third morning. He decided that he would play the Indian spinners from the crease and that he would almost totally eschew the drive. When Bedi crowded him with fielders, he took his one gamble and hit Prasanna over mid-wicket for six. Tolchard batted as though his life depended upon it and the pair were together at the close, having added 46, of which Greig had scored 19.

Shortly after midnight, he woke with a raging fever. He bathed and the bedclothes were changed in an effort to bring him some comfort. At three in the morning, Bernard Thomas was summoned and offered what medication he could. He suggested that Tony try to forget about time and to get as much rest as possible. It was advice that was difficult to follow. He ate breakfast under instruction from Bernard Thomas, for he needed the sustenance to see him through the day. He spoke as little as possible and sat in the dressing-room, drinking a considerable amount of liquid that Thomas prescribed and taking the occasional tablet.

Tony Greig was both moved and lifted by the crowd who stood and cheered as he and Tolchard took the field. The Indians would have been happy to claim Tony Greig as their own from the first moment they saw him. He gives credit to Roger Tolchard, who hit 67 before being bowled by Bedi. Tolchard's attitude and concentration was both a help and an inspiration to his skipper. The pair added 142 in four hours twenty minutes. It was a partnership which virtually decided the match.

Greig's part was far from over. He batted throughout the day and ended on 94. It was not a pretty innings to watch, nor was it one in character, but no captain of England has played an innings more important to his side. He played the spinners from the crease, taking an off-stump guard to Bedi and often using his pads for balls pitched just outside leg stump. The ball was turning and lifting, and batting was far from easy, but in intense heat and with a temperature above one hundred, Tony Greig survived, and with Old proving another brave partner, England were 130 ahead by the end of the third day.

At the end of the day, Greig was totally exhausted, but he remembers vividly the encouragement given to him by the rest of the side and the support of Willis and manager Ken Barrington, in particular. He later described 3 January 1977, as 'one of the longest, most uncomfortable and most fulfilling days of my life'.

The rest day gave Greig a chance to recuperate, and on the fourth day he duly completed his century before falling leg-before to Prasanna. His century occupied 415 minutes and was the second slowest for England in Test history. It was an innings of immense application. As he had answered the fire of the Australian and West Indian pace bowlers with fire, so he had answered one of the greatest spin attacks world cricket has seen with patience and resolve.

He followed his century with two wickets as India were bowled out for 181 and England went on to claim a famous victory by ten wickets.

During the course of his 103, Tony Greig became the first England player to score 3,000 runs and take 100 wickets in Test cricket. Only Botham has achieved a similar record for England, just as Botham is the only other England player to have hit a century and taken five wickets in a Test innings.

Tony Greig was an all-rounder of world class. He was engaging and brave, and no cricketer was ever more combative. 'Temperamentally', wrote Peter Walker, 'he seemed to grow even more in stature, if that were possible, when England faced a crisis.'

He was again to the fore when England beat India by 200 runs in the Third Test in Calcutta. This was the first time that India had ever lost the first three Tests of a home rubber, and it was England's first victory in a Test series in India since Jardine's side had won by two Tests to nil in 1933-34.

India won the Fourth Test, and the Fifth was drawn so that England took the series by three to one. The tour was a total triumph for Greig, who had led England out of the darkest of periods, and the successes that were to come in the next few years owed much to what he created at this time. 'England's superiority,' wrote Dicky Rutnagur, 'came from dedication to the task on hand, zest, determination, a thoughtful approach and a bond of brotherhood between the players. They were inspired by their flamboyant and articulate captain, Tony Greig, and team management, under Ken Barrington, must also take credit for the excellent spirit and discipline that prevailed. Greig's charisma enabled him to extract maximum effort from his players.'

Ray Illingworth ranks Tony Greig highly among Test captains, although he felt that Greig had technical deficiencies and that there were better readers of the game. Illingworth spoke of him as being 'one of the most imposing and influential captains in the history of English cricket'. He went on, 'The true gauge of his charismatic personality was the great spirit he instilled into a side that tasted failure before success. Anyone can foster good morale in a winning team. Greig revelled in the pressure-cooker atmosphere of top sport, and it was typical that many of his greatest triumphs were moulded out of adversity. His seven-hour century in the 1977 Calcutta Test against India, when he batted with a temperature of 104, was characteristic. Players respond to that kind of selfless determination.'

That innings at Calcutta was memorable in that it was Tony Greig's eighth and last century in Test cricket. From India, the England party moved, via Sri Lanka, to Australia in order to play in the celebratory Centenary Test match in Melbourne.

At the team dinner, the evening before the match, Greig discussed policy with his players and told them that he was contemplating putting Australia in if he won the toss. Bob Willis responded that such an action would be sheer lunacy, but Willis later generously admitted that it was he who had been the 'lunatic'. Greig's decision proved to be absolutely right. The pitch was more in favour of the batsmen as the game progressed.

It was a colourful, festive occasion. Australia were bowled out for 138, but England made only 95. A bustling century from Rodney Marsh took Australia to 419 for 9 declared in their second innings, and, despite Randall's 174, England were beaten by 45 runs. The result was identical to the result of the first Test match between Australia and England played at Melbourne one hundred years earlier.

During the tea interval on the final day, the teams were presented to Her Majesty the Queen and to the Duke of Edinburgh. There were many great cricketers of the past at the match which was a wonderful celebration of Test cricket. It was the fourteenth time that Tony Greig had captained England, and the fifth time he had tasted defeat in that role. It was also to be the last time that he took the field as England's captain.

The Packer Affair

IN APRIL 1977, some weeks after the Centenary Test match, Lee Irvine, the South African batsman who played for Essex for two seasons, 1968 and 1969, mentioned in an after-dinner speech in his native country that a form of exhibition cricket was being planned for the following season in Australia, for the purpose of wide television coverage. The comment was widely reported in the South African newspapers, but it was given little notice elsewhere, the news being interpreted as reference to some series of matches involving a side like the Cavaliers or the future Lord's Taverners.

By the beginning of May, however, there were rumbles from Australia that something big was afoot, and on Sunday, 8 May most of the leading cricket correspondents from the national Press congregated at the County Ground at Hove aware that news of great importance was to be revealed. They were handed a statement by Stanley Allen, the Sussex secretary, which had been issued by Tony Greig. The statement read:

'There is a massive cricket project involving most of the world's top players, due to commence in Australia this winter. I am part of it, along with a number of English players. Full details and implications of the scheme will be officially announced in Australia later this week.'

Within a few days it was learned that some thirty-five of the world's leading cricketers from England, Australia, Pakistan, West Indies and South Africa had contracted to play a series of international matches during the next Australian season, and these matches would be televised on Channel Nine which was owned by Kerry Packer. At that time, little was known in England of Kerry Packer, but what was seen immediately as a threat by him to the established order of cricket caused him to be branded as a wealthy, self-seeking individual whose sole aim in life was to destroy traditional cricket and its attendant virtues. It is not difficult for the Press to manipulate public opinion. In World War Two, when Russia was an ally, Stalin was consistently presented with a warm, bushy, upturned moustache, the image of 'Uncle Joe'. It was only later that the moustache drooped into the threatening bear.

Packer was always interested in sport, his father had been responsible for Australian challenges for the Americas Cup, and he was a powerful newspaper and television network owner. In 1975, his Channel Nine network had carried out marketing analysis and had come to the conclusion that the greatest potential lay in sports programmes. They saw that such programmes would command large audiences and huge sponsorship if they had guaranteed exclusive coverage which would bring in the necessary advertising to cover the costs.

Accordingly, Packer wrote to the Australian Cricket Board, stating that his company wanted to bid for the exclusive rights to cover the Australian-West Indies series, 1975-76. His letter was acknowledged, but the Board sold rights, not exclusive, to the Australian Broadcasting Commission and gave Packer no opportunity to make a bid.

Undeterred, Packer offered half a million Australian dollars for the sole rights of the following year's series, Australia-Pakistan, and for Sheffield Shield matches. The offer was part of a much larger bid which would have been lucrative for Australian cricket and which would have given Channel Nine exclusive rights to televise Test cricket in Australia for the next five years. The Australian Broadcasting Commission was again given the contract, although their offer was much lower and was not for exclusive coverage. There was talk of the 'special relationship' between the Board and the ABC. In the wake of his second rejection, Packer, along with other business men and entertainers, conceived the idea of World Series Cricket, one of their objects being to find more money for top cricketers to bring them closer to other world sportsmen.

It is worth considering the financial state of cricket in England at this time, and the attitudes to finance. The County Championship had no sponsor until Schweppes in 1977, and Test cricket was to have no sponsorship until Cornhill Insurance took over the responsibility in 1978. This was as a direct reaction to the Packer revolution. In 1969, Ben Brocklehurst, the lively and imaginative owner of *The Cricketer*, had put forward the idea of the cricket World Cup. It took six years before his idea was acted upon, and only then because it was prompted from another area. The original response from the TCCB to the suggested competition was that they did not feel that it should be sponsored, as that might lessen the dignity of the competition, and this was said at a time when cricket had just reported debts of close on a quarter of a million pounds with little sign of being able to clear those debts. Until late into the Eighties, the marketing department of the TCCB was run by a handful of dedicated people from what appeared to be a reconstructed broom cupboard on the first floor of the pavilion at Lord's.

The main problem regarding Packer's World Series Cricket was the way in which it was presented in England. It was Australian in origin, revolved around an Australian domestic dispute, was therefore 'colonial' and dubious in taste and virtue. It fell almost solely to Tony Greig to break the news of it, to explain it and justify it. He was immediately regarded with deep suspicion. He was, after all, South African. He had always been demonstrative and aggressive on the field, and he had even challenged the umpire's decision at Madras on his first tour of India. He had also, unforgivably, said that he would make the West Indians 'grovel'.

Even Henry Blofeld could write: 'Controversy, be it of his own making or not, has followed Greig closely, and he has always answered any criticism with an articulate form of self-confidence. He argues well, he is plausible, and it is never long before he has managed to justify his rasher actions to others as well as to himself. While Greig's record for England shows unarguably that he has been a very great asset as a player, his impulsive nature has always made him a potential liability.'

What was now ignored was that he had led England out of a period of darkness and despair. It was said that he had used and violated the position of England captain for his own advantage, but he had no contact with Packer until after the conclusion of the Centenary Test in Melbourne. The office of captain of England gave no security of tenure. He knew that there were many in authority who had wanted Brearley to take the side to India, that there were still those who resented his appointment and that, as Illingworth confirmed later, 'inside the game he had many critics'. He had been a popular choice who had sought advice from those he respected in the game, men like Close and Illingworth, and that is not always easy for authority to forgive.

Looking back over more than a decade, one can see how badly the idea of World Series Cricket was presented. It was seen as a deliberate attempt to sabotage Test cricket by presenting alternative international cricket at the same time. It was a challenge to Test cricket, but Packer had contacted the cricketing authorities of the world with an offer of compromise, only to be ignored. Packer created World Series Cricket as a business promotion to further his media interests.

Promotional poster for the Packer cricket 'circus'.

Greig and the other cricketers concerned joined him for financial reasons and to secure their futures. Knott, Lloyd, Underwood and others were to come through unscathed. They were to continue their Test careers, be honoured by Buckingham Palace and become managers and selectors of Test sides. Greig did not come through unscathed. He was identified as the spokesman for the revolutionaries, and it was he who was to take the brunt of the criticism and villification.

When Sandy and Joyce came to England for Tony's *This is Your Life* in 1977 they learned of his involvement. Sandy was not pleased. Not that he was against the idea of World Series Cricket, but he was not a man who wanted to be consulted about a major project after the event. There was a temporary breach, but it was soon healed and Sandy later helped Tony in his business venture in Australia. Other breaches were to be longer lasting. As Richie Benaud also found, there were 'friendships' that were broken that have never been repaired.

The irony is that the 'crime' that Greig and the other cricketers who joined World Series Cricket committed was to accept an offer of more money for doing their work than their current employers were prepared to offer them. It was a 'crime' of which those who run the game have been 'guilty' for much of their lives. Inevitably, they have been men secure in business firms in the City, the recipients of large salaries. For them, however dedicated, cricket could always be viewed as an amateur pastime. For those who earned a living from the game, like Arnold Bakewell who played for England in the Thirties, was involved in a car accident and became destitute, it was a means of survival. In 1977, the fee for an overseas tour with England was £3,000. Packer offered five to six times that amount. In the wake of Packer, the TCCB found that they were able to pay £1,000 for appearing in a Test match as opposed to the £210 a player had received previously. They were, in effect, following the tried business principle, still very much in existence, pay an employee as little as possible until he threatens to leave for a rival firm and then meet their offer and give him a bigger car. As Ric Sissons has pointed out in his splendid study of the professional cricketer, *The Players,* the earnings of the average county professional have doubled in *real terms* since the Packer Revolution. On the county circuit, you would find it difficult to find anyone who has a word of criticism for Tony Greig. Those old enough to remember know what a transition his actions brought about.

The Cricket Council called an emergency meeting for 13 May 1977, and issued a statement after the meeting to the effect that Greig was not to be considered for the England captaincy for the series against Australia that summer, for 'his action has inevitably impaired the trust which existed between the cricket authorities and the Captain of the England side'. It was a trust, of course, which was well understood by Denness, Illingworth and Lewis, and by Chapman, Carr and Jardine before them, and which would later be understood by Fletcher, Willis, Gower, Gatting and Chris Cowdrey. Freddie Brown added, 'The captaincy of the England team involves close liaison with the selectors in the management, selection and development of England players for the future and clearly Greig is unlikely to be able to do this for his stated intention is to be contracted elsewhere during the next three winters.' This was a sounder argument.

The debate continued. Packer came to England to discuss the position, but his demand that he should be allowed to tender for *exclusive* television rights in Australia from 1981, when the contract between the Australian Board and the ABC expired, was unacceptable although such exclusivity has not proved a barrier in recent years if the offer has been high enough.

There was a feeling rampant in May that the players who were contracted to Packer should not be picked for the England side to play Australia. This was, to say the least, irrational, as the majority of the Australian side were to join World Series Cricket. The TCCB ended speculation on 14 June when they issued a statement saying that the selection committee would 'pick England sides this summer strictly on merit'.

One feels that Mike Brearley played no little part in this decision. He admired and respected Greig, just as he admired and respected Knott and Underwood, and he wanted these men in his side. He has been ever quick to remind people of the debt that England owed to Tony Greig. Eight years on, he was to write of his experiences as vice-captain under Greig thus:

'I enjoyed the job, and was struck by how simple it is compared with being the man who has to act and "take the can". I was a relative novice at the start of the tour (having played only two Tests, both against

West Indies the previous summer). Naturally, Greig turned for advice, in the first instance, to Knott and Fletcher, both excellent advisers and highly experienced tourists. I had to learn, and to wait until he rated my opinion highly enough to consult me regularly. In the course of that trip, our mutual respect was much enhanced, and the upheaval of the months that followed, in which the idea of World Series Cricket was spawned and Greig lost the England captaincy to me, did not damage it. In 1977, he was willing, and able, to offer me in return the solid support of his advice and criticism.'

To Greig, Brearley gave credit for the fact that England were more restrained than the Australians in the field. It was Greig's insistence, when captain, that the team carried on without fuss whenever a decision went against them; Brearley stressed that this attitude must continue. It was Greig who, on the eve of the First Test, reminded the side that it was more of a sin to get out for 40 than for a duck.

Brearley believed Greig to be the best slip fielder with whom he ever played, but, above all, he felt that much of the credit for the spirit in the side and the victory over Australia belonged to Tony Greig. 'When he was dismissed as captain, he might have shown more resentment, or have been only moderately co-operative. In fact, he could not have been more helpful. He and I dined together during the Tests. During the summer we became closer, personally, than we had been during the four months abroad.'

It is also interesting to note that, on the eve of the First Test, Brearley dreamed, amongst things, of Tony Greig. He recorded, in *The Return of the Ashes*, that the dream was easy enough to interpret. 'There is nothing unusual, for instance, in feeling a certain insecurity about such an exposed position as England cricket captain, and since all my Test matches had been played under Tony Greig, a powerful personality, the image of me anxiously trotting after him is not altogether out of place.'

The First Test, the Jubilee match at Lord's, was drawn. Greig came in at 11 for 3. He was confronted by pace rather than the spin against which he had so patiently built innings in India. He was bowled by Pascoe as he tried to drive. Brearley believed, 'It's the Old Adam — he has to make things happen, stride high, assert himself, and smash an early four.' He was out for five, but in the second innings, he hit 91.

He followed this with 76 at Old Trafford, where England won by nine wickets. The Third Test was at Trent Bridge. Boycott returned to Test cricket with a century, Ian Botham played for England for the first time, and there was victory over Australia in Nottingham for the first time in forty-seven years.

The Fourth Test was played at Headingley. At the eve-of-match dinner, the players discussed an initiative that had been put forward by a business man, David Evans, later to be known as a less than popular chairman of Luton Town and as an outspoken supporter of Margaret Thatcher. He had found three other business men, and between them, they were willing to give £90,000 to the England team. The money was to go to the nine players who were not contracted to Packer. Typically, Brearley insisted that all twelve players were to have a share; equally typically, Greig said that he welcomed the money, but that he would much rather it were divided nine ways, than for there to be no money at all.

England regained the Ashes at Headingley. Tony Greig hit 43 and dismissed the Australian openers, McCosker and Davis, when the tourists were forced to follow-on. England won by an innings and there was rejoicing throughout the land. Amidst the jubilation and celebration in the dressing-room, there was some unease, for there was a rumour that the Packer players would be omitted from the last Test now that the series had been won. Brearley was angry at this suggestion and he pursued his point vigorously with the other selectors. He was more than satisfied when it was decided, unanimously, 'to include Packer players who had contributed so richly to England's successful summer'.

The final Test, at The Oval, was an anticlimax in every way. Nearly twelve hours were lost to rain, and the match was drawn. Tony Greig was out for nought, and his last contribution to Test cricket was when he had David Hookes caught behind by Alan Knott, a most faithful disciple, for 85.

Tony Greig had played in 58 consecutive Test matches. He had hit 3,599 runs, average 40.43, made eight centuries and taken 87 catches. His 141 wickets had cost 32.20 runs each and had been taken with both medium-pace and off-breaks. It is a record which places him among the top seven or eight all-rounders in the history of Test cricket. It was a short, brilliant career, and when it ended he was still two months from his thirty-first birthday.

Considering the pressure that he was under, it was remarkable that Greig achieved so much at Test and county level in 1977. There was optimism at Hove. Imran Khan, eager to play under such a dynamic leader as Tony Greig, joined Sussex from Worcestershire, not without dissenting voices, and there was a strength and confidence that the south coast had not witnessed for many seasons. The year was to end with feelings of some regret at what might have been. Jack Arlidge was to sum it up in *Wisden*.

'Greig's spirits did not flag and although his batting and bowling figures, by his standards, were disappointing, he gave his usual tremendous effort and his magnificent fielding, in particular, set an inspiring lead. He had tried to establish a new attitude of mind in Sussex cricket, to be good winners rather than good losers. This fighting spirit enabled the side to pull round and finish a respectable eighth in the championship table and win nine John Player matches to be up among the leading clubs. This was reasonably satisfactory, but we were left to ponder what might have been without the Packer business.'

After only four matches the following season, in which he had no success, Tony Greig asked to be released from his contract and relieved of the captaincy. The club agreed to his request but they were mindful to thank him for his services, and, as with England, it was his legacy rather than his achievement in office that was his greatest gift. He brought spirit and joy back to Sussex cricket and there are many who have not forgotten that.

That his end with Sussex was to be a whimper rather than the bang with which it had begun was an inevitable part of the pressure to which he was subjected in 1977.

By July, Kerry Packer had more than fifty of the world's leading cricketers under contract for his World Series Cricket. On 26 July, the ICC formulated three main resolutions:

1. No player, who after 1 October 1977 has played or has made himself available to play in a match previously disapproved by the Conference, shall thereafter be eligible to play in any Test match without the express consent of the Conference, to be given only on the application of the governing body for cricket of his country.
2. Any match arranged or to be arranged by J.P.Sports (PTY) Ltd, Mr Kerry Packer, Mr Richie Benaud or associated companies or persons, to take place in Australia or elsewhere between 1 October 1977, and 31 March 1979, is disapproved.
3. Matches are liable to be disapproved if so arranged as to have the probable result that invitations to play in such matches will conflict with invitations

which have been or may be received to play in first-class matches.

This was followed on 10 August by an announcement of the TCCB's sub-rules which were aimed at implementing the ICC resolutions. The second of these rules stated:

'No county shall be entitled to play in any competitive county cricket match, any cricketer who is and remains precluded from playing a Test match on the above grounds (*ie — appearing in a disapproved Packer match*) before the expiration of a period of two years immediately following the date of the last day of the last match previously disapproved by the ICC in which he has played or made himself available to play.

What legal advice was given the TCCB before they formulated this ruling will ever remain one of the mysteries of the universe. It was not to save them from defeat in the High Court.

On 26 September 1977, the hearing began before Mr Justice Slade of the cases of *Greig and others v Insole and others,* and of *World Series Cricket Pty Ltd v Insole and others.* It will always be unfortunate that the cases had to personalized in this way, naming Tony Greig as leader of the players and Doug Insole as chairman of the Board. The hearing lasted 31 days. The crux of the matter was the writ issued by Greig, Proctor and Snow against the TCCB in that in their new ruling, they were guilty of an unlawful restraint of trade. Justice Slade found for the players and for World Series Cricket in both actions. Whilst he had sympathy that the cricket authorities believed that they had the best interests of the game at heart, he concluded that their new rules 'if implemented, substantially restrict the area in which it will be open to professional cricketers to earn their livings. It is common ground that the rules of an association which seek substantially to restrict the area in which a person may earn his living in the capacity in which he is qualified to do so, are in restraint of trade.'

Justice Slade agreed with Greig, Procter and Snow that they were being unjustly denied the right to work, and that Snow and Greig would, in effect, be driven out of first-class cricket.

More importantly, Justice Slade refuted the moral criticism that had been levelled against the players, a fact which has been discreetly ignored by those who have continued to condemn Greig over the years.

'A professional cricketer needs to make his living as much as any other professional man. I think it is straining the concept of loyalty too far for authorities such as the defendants to expect him to enter into a self-denying ordinance not to play cricket for a private promoter during the winter months, merely because the matches promoted could detract from the future profits made by the authorities, who are not themselves willing or in a position to offer him employment over the winter or to guarantee him employment in the future.'

This lack of security and of guaranteed winter employment had been touched upon by the Kent chairman when Underwood and Knott had approached him early in the season regarding their involvement with Packer. He had intimated that Kent could have no objections as they offered their players no employment in the close season. That men like Knott and Underwood saw the chance to associate themselves with Packer's project as a godsend is undeniable. Underwood had always been worried as to what he would do when his playing career was over, since he had no qualifications and had been able to save little from a limited income.

England's cricketers' earnings had kept pace neither with inflation nor with the general increase in earnings enjoyed by other workers. In the mid-Seventies, one county professional with no prospect of playing for England could complain that the only increase he and his colleagues had seen had come solely from sponsorship; nothing had come in a wage increase from his county.

Such concern over money was, of course, anathema to some who governed the game and to some who wrote about it. It was rather un-English to talk about money, and one can cite the case of Anthony Trollope, one of the finest of novelists, who forfeited much of his standing in the eyes of literary critics when he dared to list in his autobiography how much each of his novels had brought him in revenue. This implication that an author had written the *Barchester* and *Palliser* novels with an eye to profit as well as to art caused concern to some. The formation of World Series Cricket did much the same for several people in the cricket world.

Alan Hill could write in *The Family Fortune*: 'It is sad this combative, exciting, inspirational cricketer should have chosen to pitch himself and lead others into a sordid squabble. As the leader of the breakaway group, Greig may be sincere in his desire to give financial security to his contemporaries. But he has revealed a Machiavellian streak which cricket followers, if not the rank and file county player, will find hard to understand. By his actions Greig may have forfeited the esteem of cricket.' Is it really so dreadful for the 'rank and file' to want to earn a decent living from what they do, even if they are lucky enough to be paid for doing something they love?

A more balanced, but equally critical assessment of Greig came from E.W.Swanton, a writer to whom all owe something and whose opinion should always be considered. In *Barclay's World of Cricket*, he wrote of Greig, 'There is scarcely an episode in English cricket history more poignant or depressing than the rise and fall of Tony Greig. In the early months of 1977, as

England's captain, he had reached a pinnacle of achievement and popularity granted to few. Within a matter of weeks the news of his clandestine alliance with a man bent on disrupting the traditional structure of the game meant his removal from the captaincy. The following year his links with Sussex were severed, and he departed for Australia and employment in the high-powered and questionable "marketing" of the game on which he made such an auspicious impact only 11 years before.

'One way and another the game at this point had reached a high point of prosperity, both from the financial angle and in terms of public interest. No one grudged the high income that the top players, and in particular the England captain, were beginning to earn. Then, out of the clearest of blue skies, came the revelation of Kerry Packer's secret intrusion into the cricket world, wherein Greig, while England's captain, had played a crucial recruiting part.

'When the damage that he and some of his contemporaries did to the game is assessed, his merits as an all-rounder also deserve to be remembered.'

There are three points here which deserve some attention. The first is that the 'questionable marketing' showed a path which the TCCB have been happy to follow, albeit at a snail's pace. Packer's intrusion into Australian cricket has given the game in that country a healthier financial base and a wider public interest than it had before.

In 1977, the game was certainly in better shape than it had been a decade earlier, but the players, as we have evidenced, can hardly be said to have been earning high incomes. As Derek Underwood pointed out, 'For me the security offered by the Packer contract is vital. In this one season I can double the income I collected in the tax year April 1976 to April 1977, when I played a series against the West Indies, had a full season for Kent and went on a four-month tour of India.'

151

Allied to this increase in earnings, as Ric Sissons indicated, was the realization that the involvement of companies like Cornhill Insurance and Packer's Channel Nine showed that substantial corporate sponsorship could be found for the benefit of cricket and that some of the income could be passed on to players in the form of better wages, conditions and prize money. The significant increase in the counties' wage bills was met, over the next decade, by the increased commercialization of first-class cricket. It has not always been easy to accept, but it is doubtful whether the game would have survived without it.

And what damage had been done? There has been an unhealthy increase in the number of one-day internationals in Australia, but the game in England remains structurally the same although there are moves to insist on four-day Championship cricket which, one feels, would have a more disastrous effect on the game than anything conceived by Packer.

The reaction to the whole Packer affair, of course, was similar to the emotion engendered whenever a Fourth Division football club is threatened with extinction. Twenty thousand people sign petitions and parade the streets that it must be saved, yet only twelve hundred of them a week have bothered to pay to watch the club for the past ten years.

It is ironic that, some years after the establishment of World Series Cricket, Graham Gooch led a rebel tour to South Africa which had been planned in cloak and dagger fashion that made the Packer affair look naïve and that Gooch, having served his suspension from Test cricket, returned to become captain of England and to receive the OBE.

There was to be no such rehabilitation for Tony Greig. World Series Cricket virtually signalled the end of his career. He would never be the one to look for alibis or excuses, but one feels that the pressure, the criticisms and the broken friendships inevitably took

Hero or villain? Tony Greig under World Series Cricket floodlights.

Tony Greig catches David Hookes off the bowling of Derek Underwood in the final 'Super Test' in February 1979.

their toll of him. He achieved very little in the two seasons of World Series Cricket. He scored a meagre 71 runs in four 'Super Tests', took seven wickets at more than forty runs apiece and fared little better in the one-day matches.

When peace broke out, others were to return to Test cricket; he was not. When West Indies tasted defeat Clive Lloyd and his men were quickly restored to favour and won the Prudential World Cup. Brearley insisted on recalling Alan Knott to the England side in 1981,

154

A relaxed moment during the Rest of the World v Australia game at Melbourne Stadium.

Clive Rice and Tony Greig after their side's success at Sydney in May 1979.

even though the Kent wicketkeeper had stated that he would never again make himself available for a tour. He was later to become an adviser on England selection. By that time, Greig had settled in Sydney.

The 'crime' that Greig committed was to be part of a group that attempted to bring cricket into the twentieth century, and such wrenches are never comfortable. Richie Benaud, one who played a leading part in the revolution, has written: 'There are some who would wish the game of cricket always to be conducted as in the local parish, with the thatched roof pavilion sheltering the scorer, the scones and the strawberry jam, dainty salmon and cucumber sand-wiches and weak tea between innings, and instant

156

The Rest of the World side confer at the fall of an Australian wicket.

excommunication or possibly execution for the most trifling misdemeanour. I cheerfully confess not to be in that august company. It is, I hasten to say, a delightful way of life but it doesn't work.' At least, as Benaud might have added, not in the professional game, which needs professional salaries, professional standards, and, in the Eighties and Nineties, professional marketing. This may be a sadness, but it is not the fault of cricket, rather one should blame a world in which the supermarket philosophy has been encouraged to dominate and where the insensitivity of the world of commerce reigns supreme.

Mike Brearley suggested a colourful sustained metaphor of Greig and the Packer affair.

Tony Greig with collar upturned, a familar pose.

'The whole story has epic, almost mythological elements in it that I find fascinating. Tony Greig, the Prince Charming, the Golden Giant who comes from afar (South Africa) to set right our tottering State (English cricket). Like Oedipus (without the limp) he rids the state of the bane that sits upon its walls (we win in India). Does he, now, outreach himself by challenging the gods? Is this his humbris? Prometheus, who stole fire from the gods for men, spent many years chained to a rock in Asia Minor with an eagle pecking at his liver; Greig's banishment will not, we presume, be as uncomfortable, though I do like the image of him playing Faustus to Mr Packer's Mephistopheles.

'Is Greig, in this egregious melodrama, Prometheus or Satan?'

Alan Knott has no doubt that he is Prometheus. In more mundane terms, he believes that Greig has done more for professional cricket than any other man.

After Packer

MORE than a decade after the Packer Affair, Tony Greig gave an interview to Simon Barnes of *The Times* in which he reflected, reluctantly, on the events that caused so much bitterness in 1977 and 1978. 'I think I was perhaps a bit too inclined to justify what I had done. For there is no doubt that I joined World Series Cricket for Tony Greig. For my family and my future. We've all got a right to do that.

'There was nothing permanent about the England captaincy! All the people who had held the captaincy before me at that time had believed they were going to hold the job for a long time. But they didn't. So I didn't feel guilty about that aspect.

'I was one of those guys selected for the project and I was able to negotiate a future for myself. I wasn't that strung up about the whole thing, it wasn't any big deal for me until various people in the cricket hierarchy came up to me, incapable of doing anything other than being totally nasty.'

Greig was hurt. He is a sensitive man, one who has had his share of care. He was not one born for a tranquil life. The concern for the future is more difficult to understand for those who have the security of an index-linked pension. Few actors, few cricketers have such security and live with the constant fear that 'it could all end tomorrow', which explains Gooch's trip to South Africa and Gielgud's appearances in television thrillers of industrial espionage unworthy of a man of his great talent. Sir Neville Cardus and John Arlott are two other men of talent who, at times in their lives, expressed concern as to what the future might hold.

The concern was, and is, deep-rooted in Tony Greig, although one would feel that now he has little cause for worry.

Ian Greig tells of how, when Tony's son Mark came to stay with him and his wife Cheryl in Surrey, he was provided with a sum of money by his father which he had to budget carefully to cover the cost of fares and entrance fees to such places as museums. Ian insisted that there were occasions when he wanted to pay for his nephew, but the boy was adamant that his father had set him a task which he should carry out fully. It was a lesson in precautionary values.

Tony Greig had not intended to leave England, nor county cricket, when he first became contracted to Packer, but events made his departure almost inevitable. He had no desire to continue in first-class cricket until his forties, and the pressures on him over World Series Cricket accelerated his retirement. His decision to leave England and settle in Australia was brought about by the hostility which he met and, particularly, by some petty acts of vindictiveness against his children. He is, however, a forgiving man, and these are things he does not care to dwell upon any more.

If he did not thrive as a player in World Series Cricket, he still made a considerable contribution to the project. Richie Benaud asserts that World Series Cricket was fun, that it was the busiest time of his life, that 'it was a time for making new friends and losing old acquaintances', and that it brought three major benefits to the game. The first of these was the improvement in pay and conditions of players *and umpires*; the second was the advent of night cricket, an exciting innovation in one-day cricket in Australia, yet to be developed in England for reasons of climate and facilities; and third, there was the introduction of the fielding circles into limited-over cricket. These have now been introduced into all forms of the one-day

Above and opposite: Practising at Melbourne with the aid of a bowling machine.

game; it was Tony Greig who presented to the governing body of World Series Cricket the idea of these circles to which a certain number of fielders are restricted until the bowler has delivered the ball. That we see them today in the Texaco Trophy, the Benson and Hedges Cup and the other one-day tournaments is a legacy of World Series Cricket and Tony Greig.

When he ceased to play he became, with the most

An unfamilar sight that was soon to become all too familar: the helmeted cricketer.

Tony Greig, the radio presenter.

able advice of his father, Sandy, a highly competent businessman, the managing director of a broking business, the Lion Insurance Company, and the managing director of an underwriting firm. These have been no sinecures. He is totally committed to the business and gives his work his unstinting energy. He is not capable of doing anything else.

He considers his work as a television commentator as something of a hobby, a relaxation that offers a contrast to his normal work without being so time

165

consuming as to distract from it. This may be true, but it has brought him a fresh legion of followers, many of whom never saw him play and to whom the 'Packer Affair' is a term as remote and as lacking in meaning as any reference to an obscure political scandal of the nineteenth century.

His work for Packer's Channel Nine was as revolutionary as had been the original concept of World Series Cricket. He took the spectator closer to the game as he not only talked about the pitch and about moisture, but also demonstrated what he was saying. For years, the layman had been told of good wickets and bad wickets, and of how they would seam or spin; Greig caressed cracks in the pitch and pointed to the level of humidity and explained how these would benefit or hinder batsman and bowler.

In his attitude to cricket, he has always been motivated by the belief that 'without the player there is no game; without the spectator there is no game'. He sees no future for a sport which alienates itself from its followers by surrounding itself with a mystique which is comprehended only by a chosen few.

When he worked for Sky Television he joined with Geoff Boycott to form the most popular of television's commentating teams, cricket's equivalent to *Saint and Greavsie*. The two men had their differences with the Establishment, and occasionally with each other, but Greig was able to sting Boycott into comment which was both illuminating and entertaining.

When it was first decided to employ Boycott, an embargo was placed upon him in that he was asked not to dwell upon his own career, his own prejudices or criticisms. Greig saw that this was robbing the man of his most valuable qualities. Boycott, like Tony Greig himself, has always been and always will be a controversial figure. Greig insisted that this suggestion of controversy was essential if Boycott was to be liberated, to be seen as someone who had comment

June 1985 and Tony Greig is deeply involved with Australia's Channel Nine Sports.

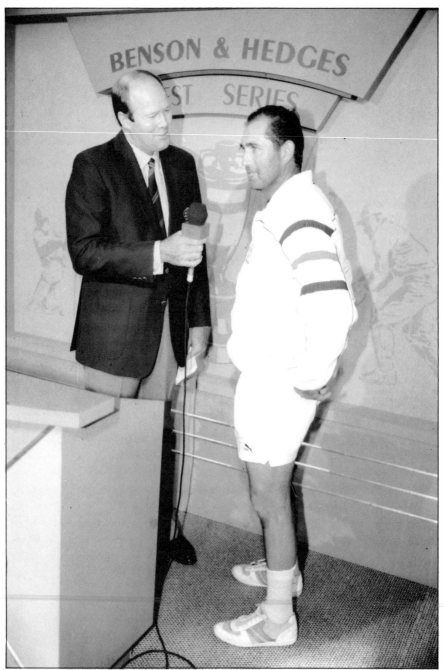

February 1991. Tony Greig interviews England skipper Graham Gooch for Channel Nine.

to make that was vital and authentic. With the liberation came a provocative double act that, allied to excellent camera work, made many say that they would find it difficult to be satisfied again with what was offered by the BBC, particularly BBC Radio. Greig himself, ever outspoken, was more scathing of radio's 'funereal' approach to the game.

For the 1991 season, Tony Greig returned to Channel Nine which had once again become part of Kerry Packer's business empire. He had been made a most handsome offer by Sky/BSkyB, but he feels a loyalty for Packer who supported him, and others, when times were less than pleasant. One of the reasons for the commercial successes of men like Kerry Packer is that they choose wisely those who are to work for them. Packer has never been disappointed in Tony Greig, and Greig has remained appreciative and loyal to Packer for all that he has done. The vast majority of professional cricketers have also remained enthusiastically appreciative of Packer and the revolution he brought about in cricket.

It is to be regretted that it was not a bloodless revolution. Many wounds have healed, but there are still scars. Tony Greig believes that enough has been said about the whole business, not all of it well informed, and that it should now be laid to rest while cricket and cricketers enjoy the benefits it brought. He is the only man to have captained England for a lengthy period not to have been made an Honorary Member of MCC.

Now the Sydney businessman, with a broken marriage, he remains a charismatic figure, courteous and affable at social gatherings, devoted to mother, brother, sisters, his children and the memory of his father whose loss he feels deeply. Simon Barnes has suggested: 'He is not the man who betrayed, or even ruined English cricket. He was just a floating object caught by the flood tide of history.' Barnes says, 'Greig is now a curiosity of history.'

He is more than that, one feels. As we have mentioned, Ray Illingworth, a man not given to praise cheaply, has called Tony Greig 'one of the most imposing and influential captains in the history of English cricket'. It seems an apt comment, although Greig would only smile wryly if you repeated it to him and say, 'I didn't really have a great philosophy of captaincy, it really was a question of leading from the front. It was all that I knew how to do. I had confidence, you see, and I thought that if there was a problem I could just do it myself. Sometimes you become aggressive in order to hide that you feel, maybe, a little insecure.'

In a medieval army, he would have been the first to climb the ladder erected to scale the enemy's walls. It would not have been a question of choice. His inner daemon would have prompted him to do it. He would have felt the scalding of the boiling oil and the bite of the first arrows. And if he did not flinch, it would not have meant that he had not felt pain.

The name of Greig will live long in the history of cricket. It is still very much alive in the zeal and honesty being brought to the game by Tony's younger brother, Ian.

Ian

TONY Greig says that one of his greatest prides is that he coached his brother, Ian, when he was a boy and helped him to develop as a cricketer. As a child, Ian idolized his big brother and he learned as much from watching Tony as he did from any verbal instruction.

One day, early in 1961, the elder of the Greig brothers was playing cricket in the garden of their Queenstown home. He was bowling quickly to one of his closest friends, Paul Ensor, who, as schoolboys will, complained that Tony was bowling too fast. In a momentary dash of madness, Tony retorted that his little brother could cope with his bowling even if Paul could not. Ian, five years old, was amongst the smaller children dotted about the garden to fetch and carry as fielders.

Paul Ensor took up Tony's challenge, scoffing at the idea that the five-year-old would stand up to such bowling. Ian was duly brought up from his fielding position, encased in pads and given the bat. Tony had no option but to go to the full extent of his run and bowl flat out. He was a formidable bowler, even at the age of fourteen, and he was very worried as to the situation he had created. He hoped he could serve up a half-volley, but he need not have worried. Ian met the brisk delivery in the middle of the bat and played the ball unerringly back to the bowler. It was his first taste of 'big' cricket, but the appetite for the game, and for sport in general, had been with him since birth. It could not have been otherwise with Sandy and Joyce as his parents.

Ian's childhood was not to pass with quite the ease

Ian Greig, the youngster who had to cope with his elder brother's bowling.

and tranquility that Tony had enjoyed. Tony and Molly were to leave home and pursue their own destinies and to be much missed by their young brother. There were to be two years in Scotland for Ian, Sally Ann and their parents, and, on returning to South Africa, Sandy was to have what was, perhaps, the most difficult period of his life.

The Greigs returned to South Africa towards the end of 1968 and Sandy first worked in East London. This meant that Ian was to go to Selborne College, but in July 1969, he was old enough to be a boarder and he followed his brother to Queen's College.

At Queen's, he soon found another hero in Ken McEwan. McEwan was the outstanding cricketer in the school and he dominated events much as Tony had done. In 1971, he was captain of the South African Schools XI. He remembers: 'I first met Ian as a young boy who had just arrived at the school. He was at the same boarding house as I was, and, being a prefect, I was entitled to a few 'fags'. Ian was one of them. I can't remember exactly what his duties were, he had to carry my books to school and return empty cake tins to my girlfriend who lived next door to his parents. He had already begun shining at sport, particularly cricket and rugby, and predictably, he carried on from there.'

When Ian had sadly said goodbye to his brother early in 1967, he had determined that he would follow the path that Tony had chosen. 'As soon as Tony did what he did, I wanted to follow.'

His school record in sport was, in fact, better than Tony's. He won a place in the first fifteen at rugby in his penultimate year at school, but the side had been a strong one, and Ian was to achieve more in the game than his brother had done. Like Tony, his cricketing prowess at school won him a place in the Border Schools' party for Nuffield Schools Week.

In 1975, the host association for the week was

Griqualand West, and the festival was staged in Kimberley. Consistent performances throughout the week, which was marred by bad weather, won Ian a place in the South African Schools' side to meet Griqualand West as the climax to the festival. Kepler Wessels, also to play for Sussex, was another in the side. Ian was down to bat at number eight, and Barnard declared with only five wickets down. He came on as first change, bowled only three overs and saw his side lose by five wickets.

It was not much of celebration from Ian's point of view, but he had won his cap, hard to fit over the shock of black hair he sported at the time, and he had played with and against senior players. Interestingly, Griqualand West were taken to victory by an exciting innings of 130 not out from their captain Trevor Jesty, later to play under Ian Greig at Surrey.

The Nuffield Schools match was played on 11 January, at the de Beers Country Club, but by then, Ian Greig was already a first-class cricketer. He and his schoolmate, Greg Hayes, were chosen for the Border side to meet Transvaal 'B' in the Currie Cup 'B' Group match in East London which began on Boxing Day, 1974. He scored 13 and 23, did not bowl and Border won by 73 runs. In the New Year match against Northern Transvaal, he hit 24. At the end of January and beginning of February, against Orange Free State at Bloemfontein, he made 8 (caught Wessels) and 0, but he bowled for the first time and claimed his first wicket in first-class cricket when he bowled Roger Prideaux, another with a Sussex connection.

The last match of the season was against Griqualand West at East London. He opened the bowling but was taken off after conceding 22 runs in two overs. Griqualand West made 276, and when Ian Greig came in Border were 151 for 6. In 103 minutes, he hit seven fours and finished with 52 not out to help his side to 243. It was an impressive maiden half-century in his first-class career.

His first season had seen him score 125 runs, average 20.83, and take three wickets at 34 runs each. He was just past his nineteenth birthday and had made a pleasing start to his first-class career. Of eight newcomers to the Border side, he and Hayes had created the best impression. It was to be Ian Greig's only season's cricket for Border for some time. Shortly after the end of the 1974-75 season, he began his twelve months period of National Service in the Army.

As a sportsman, his services were welcomed. He had played first-class cricket and been reserve for the South African Schools' rugby side. When he was posted to Kimberley he appeared for Griqualand West and led the station cricket team in the first-grade league in the city, a fact which was to have considerable bearing on his life at that time.

His period of National Service coincided with the outbreak of war in Angola. South West Africa was still a part of South Africa and those at Kimberley were the closest unit to the hostilities. With a large presence on their border, South Africa felt under threat. Greig and his colleagues had to respond to a special alarm. They were paraded at headquarters, given little information except that they were to be flown to an unspecified destination, and they were given half an hour to gather together equipment and make themselves ready to leave. The parade was dismissed, and Ian, being on the end of a file, was able to get to a telephone and call his parents to tell them what was happening. As he was phoning, the Hercules transport planes flew in.

His parents had already heard of the emergency on the radio, and Joyce was in tears. Sandy, believing perhaps that one war had been enough for any family, gave a simple instruction to his son. 'Don't try to be a hero. I'd rather have a live son than a dead hero.'

The unit paraded again and were dispatched to different vehicles which were waiting to transport them to the aircraft. Ian was sitting in a Bedford, complete with rifle and the rest of his fighting equipment, when a captain walked past who had dealings with the cricket team which had been formed after Greig and some of his colleagues had been transferred from Johannesburg to Kimberley. The captain stopped and asked, 'Greig, what are you doing there?' Ian told what had been ordered, and received the reply, 'Nonsense, get out. You've got to stay and play cricket, and so has your team got to stay.' Ian found that he was in a difficult position, for several of the conscripted cricketers were more prone to go and fight, but eventually they all stayed and played cricket as the army desired. The rest of the unit departed, leaving some twenty to thirty men in a camp which could hold 1,500.

Ian Greig was demobilized in June 1976, returned briefly to Queenstown and then caught a plane for England. A brief note in *The Cricketer* a few months earlier had suggested that he was hoping to gain a place at Cambridge. He arrived with England struggling in the Test series against West Indies, a series in which Tony had a particularly unhappy time.

Tony took Ian down to the nets at Hove and armed him with black lacrosse balls. Ian bowled at his brother off eighteen yards and he recalls Tony's words to him. 'You can give me anything. I want the ball going past me shoulder-high.'

Ian says,'I bowled at him for half an hour and then he said, "Is that the quickest you can bowl? I'll bring the stumps up to sixteen yards." I absolutely pummelled him. That was Tony's way. He motivated me in that way. He said, "We brought you over to play cricket, is this the best you can do?" I then thundered in off sixteen yards, and he was ducking and diving, and he went up to Headingley and got 116. I learned something, too.'

The tutors at Cambridge had discussed the decline in sport at the University. They decided that they would try to hold one place every year for someone who could hold his own academically and also be an advantage to the University on the sports field. For that reason, Ian Greig was awarded a place.

It was Philip Hodson, Ian's brother-in-law, who telephoned John Hopkins at Downing College and told him of Ian. Sandy flew to meet Hopkins in March, 1975, and the affair was settled.

'When I was given the place I said to dad, "Cambridge? Where's Cambridge?" ' Ian remembers.

Sandy's reply allowed no argument. He said, 'Listen, I'll sell my house, my car, everything I've got if needs be, to put you through that place.'

He was admitted whilst still in South Africa, but there was the discussion as to what he would read. He had a preference for reading physical education, but that was not a Cambridge degree, and he felt that he would settle for geography which had always been one of his best subjects and was a subject in which he was most interested. His meeting with the senior admissions tutor, John Hopkins of Downing, turned him in another direction.

Hopkins had studied Ian Greig's matriculation results and had come to the conclusion that he was best at *learning* subjects. He believed that, on this evidence, he could help the student if he read Law. A number of law books duly arrived by mail which he was asked to read before going up to Cambridge.

Greig's sole desire was to play cricket as his brother had done, but he was confronted by the problem of the four-year residential qualification. The only way he could get round this problem was to go to Cambridge, so this was a wonderful opportunity for him. If you were an undergraduate at Cambridge, you were automatically qualified to play county cricket, regardless of your nationality. However, this ruling changed just before he went up, so that the opening for him to play county cricket was no longer available. He was now faced with the four-year qualification period, but it seemed to matter little, for there was no guarantee that he would ever reach the required standard for first-class cricket in England and that playing at Cambridge would give him the chance to prove himself not only to Sussex but also to other counties. Paradoxically, much as Ian desired to emulate his brother, Tony was to envy him his years at Cambridge.

From the moment he had arrived in Brighton, he had contemplated playing for no other county but Sussex. The links had always been strong. His coaches at Selborne, where he had been from 1963 to 1966 as a day boy before the family moved to Scotland for their brief stay there, had been Colin Milburn and Albert Lightfoot. In 1969, before going to Queen's, he had been coached by Dennis Amiss, but the Queen's College ties were invariably with Sussex. There was also the constant desire to emulate Tony.

In the autumn of 1976, Ian arrived at Downing College, Cambridge, to begin his studies in Law and, more significantly, to play rugby and cricket. Ken McEwan was to say of him later: 'His achievements at Cambridge, both on and off the field, and elsewhere, were through total dedication and never giving up, but coming from the Greig family that was no surprise.' It was not to be easy. 'I always felt I was two steps behind Tony,' Ian says, 'and on my first day in Cambridge, I walked down the high street and I heard somebody say, "That's Tony Greig's brother." I had to fight to be my own man.'

Initially, his rugby was to be second-team rugger, and when his blue arrived it came as a surprise, for he was asked to play out of position on the wing. The request came from skipper Alastair Hignell and from Eddie Butler, and Ian misinterpreted it. He walked

178

away with a mixture of scorn and anger, wondering why he had been summoned to an emergency meeting to be asked to play out of position in a second-fifteen game. Then he heard Hignell say, 'Fancy turning down a blue.' And he abruptly came back to Hignell and Butler and asked for more information. Paul Parker had been forced to withdraw from the Varsity match through injury, and they felt that Greig was the man to replace him, even though he had never played on the wing.

Ian jumped at the opportunity. He received a crash course of instruction in wing play, one day of do's and don'ts from Mike O'Callaghan the former All Black. He played on the left wing for Cambridge University against Oxford and scored a try, but his side was beaten. The following year he was on the right wing. He scored a try and his side won. Ian Robertson suggested in conservation that if he played club rugby, say for London Scottish, for two seasons, he could win a place in the Scotland fifteen. He never followed that advice, and his rugby was to be restricted to his years at Cambridge, but he has continued to follow the game avidly and never misses an international at Twickenham. His cricket career was to follow a different pattern.

He won an immediate place in the University side as a freshman and shared the new ball with another freshman, Howat. He began with a duck against Leicestershire, but he had the consolation of taking the wickets of Dudleston and Balderstone in a drawn game. He had wickets, too, against Yorkshire, but it was not until the third first-class match, against Nottinghamshire, that he made his mark as a batsman, reaching double figures for the first time, in an innings of 43. Against Glamorgan he hit 61, and when Essex came to Fenner's, he made 44 and took the wicket of his former hero and senior at school, Ken McEwan, although McEwan had scored 150 before he was caught by Peter Roebuck.

He had won a place in the combined Oxford and Cambridge Universities side in the Benson and Hedges Cup and had performed well with the ball. Cambridge were certainly a stronger combination than they had been for some seasons, and Fosh, Roebuck, Hignell, Parker, Coverdale, Popplewell and Greig were all to play county cricket. That they did not beat Oxford in the Varsity match was something of a disappointment, but they had just the better of an exciting draw.

Cambridge hit 281 for 7 on the opening day, and, in an innings of 70, he showed 'the flamboyance of his brother in a stand of 90 with Parker'. He also dismissed both openers, but he had played the match under something of a cloud.

Ten days before the Varsity match, Cambridge had met Kent at Canterbury. The county hit 200, and the University were 88 for 6 when Greig, who had gone in when the fifth wicket fell for 71, was joined by Steve Coverdale, now secretary of Northamptonshire. In even time, they added 161, and Ian Greig was caught behind off Jarvis when only four runs short of what would have been a maiden first-class century. He batted for three hours and hit eleven fours. Shortly after the close of play, he received a telephone call from John Hopkins of Downing. It was to tell him that he had failed his first-year examinations. Having just missed a century by four runs, Ian was not in the best mood to receive the news that his future at Cambridge was, at the least, uncertain.

On the cricketing scene all had been well. Reviewing the Cambridge season for *Wisden*, David Hallett insisted, 'The brightest star shone in the form of Greig, the younger brother of the former England captain. He emerged into a valuable middle-order batsman. He also shared the new ball with Howat, another freshman, and was an outstanding fielder — an all-rounder in the image of his brother if with a contrasting personality.'

He had hit 394 runs, average 30.30, to finish second to Hignell in the University averages, and taken 18 wickets at 38.05 runs each. There was a vitality and enthusiasm in all that he did, but it was allied to a disarming innocence and openness. There were clear signs that he was a most capable first-class cricketer, but the problem was that his commitment to sport had so eaten into his academic studies as to make his imminent departure from Cambridge most probable.

John Hopkins came up with a solution. He negotiated that Ian should rewrite the papers before the beginning of the next academic year, that he should return to Downing at the beginning of September and prepare to resit them under his tutelage. He had phoned Sandy and told him the news, and Sandy fully supported the move. There was encouragement, too, from Tony, and, reluctantly it must be said, Ian agreed to the plan. At the second attempt, he was successful and then settled down to a second year of rugby and cricket.

He played a few games for Sussex's second eleven before returning to Cambridge and performed adequately rather than sensationally. He pays credit to the help and advice given him at the time when he was setting out on his first-class career by teammates like Alastair Hignell, Paul Parker and Peter Roebuck. They played a part in coaxing him through the period when his future at Cambridge was under threat.

Alastair Hignell, a sportsman of immense potential whose talents were never realized with Gloucestershire as fully as one felt they would be, and Paul Parker, the present captain of Sussex, were re-elected captain and secretary for the 1978 season, a most unusual honour, but it reflected the buoyancy of Cambridge cricket at the time. Sadly, Ian Greig's second year at University was a disappointment for nearly everyone.

It was a wet summer and the brief Cambridge season was badly disjointed by weather and the demands of the examination room.

Only Parker and Hignell showed anything like true form with the bat, whilst Allbrook carried the bowling on his own shoulders. Ian Greig played in the first four matches, but he was obviously well below his best. He scored only 16 runs, but he took eight wickets, including Mike Procter, when he had 3 for 73 against Gloucestershire. After the game against Leicestershire, which finished on 12 May, he went into hospital for a cartilage operation and did not play again until the Varsity match.

This was yet another disappointment. Rain washed out the second day after the first had seen Cambridge bowled out for 97. Greig made ten before being stumped. It was his highest score of the season. He sent down only three overs as Oxford were bowled out by Allbrook and Gardiner for 192, and that was his contribution to a match which ended tamely on the last day as Paul Parker scored 61 and helped Cambridge to draw. Whatever the disappointments, and however meagre Greig's season had been, at the end of the match, he was elected captain of Cambridge University Cricket Club for 1979 with Nigel Popplewell as secretary. Greig's qualities of leadership were apparent to all. He was honest, open, tactically aware, never afraid to make a positive decision and would never ask anyone to do anything that he was not prepared to do himself. These are not common qualities.

They were recognized by Sussex who, having come so close so often for nearly a decade, won the Second Eleven Championship for the first time in their history in 1978. *Wisden* commented: 'The side played consistently well all season, and credit must be given to the two captains used, C.E.Waller during the first half of the season and I.A.Greig during the second half. Both showed leadership qualities which enabled

Ian Greig, determination and endeavour.

the side to play as a professional unit.' Waller and Greig were to be reunited at The Oval some years later where, again, their talents helped revive and reshape a side.

Ian Greig returned to Cambridge in the autumn of 1978 with the single purpose of winning the Varsity match the following summer. One of his first acts was to convince the President of the Cricket Club that Cambridge University needed a coach to put them on a professional basis if they were to compete as a first-class team. He won the argument, and the man employed was Brian 'Tonker' Taylor, the former captain of Essex.

Initially, this looked an improbable choice. Taylor was a sergeant-major rather than an officer; a professional cricketer whose career had touched four decades rather than an amateur for whom the game had been a leisurely pastime. Taylor's record suggested qualities which Greig admired and which he felt the University side needed. At Essex, he had taken on the captaincy at the most difficult time in the club's history. He had taught a group of untried youngsters to be professional cricketers. He was a strong disciplinarian who insisted on standards in dress, behaviour and fitness. These were principles which Greig appreciated. He pays tribute to Taylor and gives him credit for instilling confidence into the side and the thirst for victory.

There was good fortune attending the Cambridge side in Greig's year of captaincy. In the first place, Derek Pringle, already highly regarded by Essex as an all-rounder, arrived from Felsted. There were two post-graduates of considerable talent and experience, David Surridge, a pace bowler from Hertfordshire who later played for Gloucestershire, and Nick Cooper, a steady batsman and off-break bowler who also played for Gloucestershire. A third bonus was that Crawford, a Yorkshireman who had played occasionally in 1978 as a batsman but had not won a blue, emerged as a medium-pace bowler well worth his place in the side.

The preparations for the Varsity match were not helped by the wretched weather. Only two and a quarter hours of play were possible on the first two days in the match against Leicestershire. Only forty minutes play were possible in three days when Surrey came to Fenner's, and it was not until their fourth first-class match of the season that the University side was able to enjoy a full day's cricket.

Ian Greig's own form was far from good, but his leadership of the side was noted with approval. He was positive in all that he did, and constantly he kept before his men that the purpose of their season was to beat Oxford at Lord's. He chose a balanced side with a varied attack which gave him the use of the off-spin of Cooper and the leg-spin of Holliday, a bowler who was to be under-used in first-class cricket, a not unusual fate for a leg-spinner. Greig saw Pringle as his key man with both bat and ball, and when the University met Combined Services at Sandhurst in the last game before the Varsity match, he gave Pringle three days off and told him to come back eager and fit, for he expected a century and five wickets from the Essex all-rounder.

Brian Taylor had treated his post as coach to the University side with the utmost seriousness and dedication. He was at Lord's by 8.30am on the morning of the Varsity match and he greeted each player as he arrived, exciting him with a sense of occasion and self-belief and sending a wave of confidence throughout the side. He then turned to Ian Greig and asked him what he was going to do if he won the toss. The day was humid, and with Lord's generally most helpful to bowlers early on the first day, Greig unhestitatingly replied that he would ask Oxford to bat first. Taylor challenged him.

'The general rule is, son, if you win the toss, you bat.'

'I'm not going to. The conditions are helpful to the bowlers, and I think we have the bowlers who can bowl them out,' Greig retorted.

'Good boy. You've thought it out. Stick by what you've decided. You've got it right, but I needed to see you knew what you were doing.'

In fact, the decision was not left to Ian Greig, for Simon Clements, the Oxford captain, won the toss and elected to bat. It was a disastrous decision. Surridge had Claughton leg-before at 19, and then Greig, moving the ball appreciably in the heavy atmosphere, sent back Clements, Moulding and Orders in quick succession, and Oxford were 28 for 4.

Greig recalls that Clements told him afterwards that the late Colin Milburn, who was the Oxford coach, did not arrive at Lord's until 12.30pm, by which time, the Dark Blues were in total disarray. He said to Clements that it was bad luck that he had lost the toss and been put in. The Oxford captain replied that he had won the toss and batted. 'You don't bat when you win the toss at Lord's on a morning like this morning,' exploded Milburn. 'You should have told us that at half-past eight this morning,' replied Clements.

Oxford were bowled out for 97 in 41 overs. The wickets were shared by Greig, 3 for 33; Surridge, 4 for 22; and Pringle, 3 for 10. By the end of the day, Cambridge were 131 for 4 and Pringle was at the wicket. There was a slight hiccup the next morning, and with six wickets down, Cambridge were only 166, a lead of 69. Pringle took charge and hit the last 49 of his 103 runs in 65 minutes. In all, he batted for three hours seven minutes and hit three sixes. Cambridge led by 205 when Greig declared as soon as Pringle reached the century his captain had asked of him. Oxford again collapsed before the bowling of Surridge, Greig,

Pringle and Popplewell, and Cambridge won by an innings and 52 runs. It was their biggest victory for 22 years and their first over Oxford for seven years.

It was a fitting climax to Ian Greig's year of captaincy. He was among the very best of Cambridge captains and his leadership was always impressive. His greatest regret is that the side broke up after that match and never again played together as a team. They were a fine unit, Pringle, Surridge, Popplewell, Cooper, Holliday, and they have met together since, but 6 July 1979, was the last time that they took the field together as a team, and Ian Greig regrets that.

His own problems did not end with leading his side to victory in the Varsity match. Once again, the time given to sport had meant that the time available for academic study was very limited, and he was unsuccessful in his final examinations. There was, however, much sympathy for him from others as well as from John Hopkins. It was generally recognized that he had been the main force in the rejuvenation of sport in the University, and it was felt that he should not be allowed to suffer because of this commitment. Once more arrangements were made that he should resit the papers before the beginning of the next academic year. He was successful and passed out into the world as a graduate of Cambridge University. More important, he had established that he was his own man.

At Queen's College, he had inherited Tony's nickname of 'Washies', and in his early days at Cambridge, he was always referred to in newspaper reports and elsewhere as Tony Greig's younger brother. Now he was a double blue at Cambridge and the man who had led the cricket team with perception and intelligence to a long-awaited victory over Oxford. Whether or not he would be able to fulfil his ambition of proving himself in county cricket and earning his living as a professional cricketer still remained uncertain.

Rise and Fall

IAN Greig's playing record at Cambridge is not amongst the most impressive of those who have represented that University. In three seasons, he had appeared in 22 first-class matches, hit 669 runs, average 23.89, and taken 32 wickets at 38.90 runs each. These were not figures that would have attracted attention, had it not been for the total commitment and dedication of the young man himself, the undoubted potential that had not yet been fully realized and the impression that he made on all those who met him.

At Sussex, however, there was no general consensus of opinion that he was worthy of an extended contract, and the man who fought for him, staking his own reputation in the process, was Tony Buss, so long an ally of the Greigs. Buss was the county coach in 1977 and 1978. He was one of Sussex's finest servants and an outstanding coach, but he was followed, after twenty-five years of faithful service, by Stewart Storey who captained the second eleven in 1979 when Ian Greig hit his first century as a Sussex player.

It was in 1979 that Ian appeared for the county side for the first time. At the end of August, he was in the team for the John Player Sunday League game against Hampshire at Southampton. He batted number five, scored 6 and did not bowl. That winter he went to South Africa and played one game for Border. It was against Western Province 'B' at Newlands, and he returned career-best bowling figures of 5 for 60 in the home side's first innings.

The transition from second eleven to first-eleven cricket is not an easy one as many professionals and young men of talent have discovered, and Ian Greig did not find his first season with Sussex to be anything but hard. Perhaps the pressure on him at Hove was even greater than it had been at Cambridge. He was the brother of a former county captain and England captain who, in the eyes of some, was notorious for having 'betrayed' English cricket. As at Cambridge, Ian was determined that he would not live in his brother's shadow, that he would be his own man.

Arnold Long gave him his first Championship match, against Kent at Tunbridge Wells in mid-June. He made 1 and 32 and took the wicket of John Shepherd. He held his place for the rest of the season and in his second Championship game, against Somerset at Hove, he hit 53, helping Colin Wells add 131 in 24 overs. By the end of the season, he had scored 366 runs and, sparingly used, taken 11 wickets. The impressive factor was that he bowled, batted and fielded with such obvious enthusiasm. It was an infectious quality, and he became a favourite with spectators. This was particularly so on Sunday afternoons, when his fielding caught the eye and he always appeared to be doing 'something' in the game.

If Greig's first season as a Sussex player, 1980, had suggested that Tony Buss' judgement was correct and that the young all-rounder would become a good county cricketer, his second season intimated that was a conservative prediction. Sussex have never won the County Championship, and they have never come closer to winning it than they did in 1981. They beat Yorkshire by eight wickets in the last match of the season at Hove, only to learn that Nottinghamshire, having beaten Glamorgan in two days on the doubtful Trent Bridge pitch, had taken the title by the margin of two points.

The crucial game had been the one at Trent Bridge in mid-August when Sussex, having scored 208, bowled out the home side for 102. Sussex collapsed for 144 in their second innings, saved only from humiliation by 43 from Greig and 42 from Gould. Nottinghamshire began the last day requiring 251 to win with all their wickets intact. They slipped to 73 for 3, but Hassan and Rice added 101. Barclay was jeered for using delaying tactics, but then wickets began to fall and the home side found themselves on 205 for 7 in bad light. Having previously been offered the light and declining to go off, Nottinghamshire now made for the pavilion. The Sussex players were angered that this was a breach of the laws, and that as the Nottinghamshire batsmen had earlier declined the offer to leave the field, they could not do so now, for the light was better than it had been previously. Seven of the last twenty overs were lost. When the batsmen returned, le Roux dismissed French and Cooper in successive overs, but Bore and Hemmings, offering nothing but broad, straight bats, survived the last four overs of the match to give Nottinghamshire the draw which later proved to be the decisive result in denying Sussex the Championship.

Ian Greig's contribution to Sussex's wonderful summer was outstanding. He played in every match and was awarded his county cap. He was revealed as an 'all-rounder of immense promise', 'the find of the season'. He hit 911 runs, took 76 wickets and held 14 catches in first-class matches. Against Hampshire at Hove, in the penultimate game of the season, he hit 118 not out, a maiden first-class century, and followed this with 6 for 75 and 4 for 57, so becoming only the sixth Sussex player to score a century and take ten wickets in a match. The last had been Ted Dexter in 1962. Earlier in the year, Ian Greig had routed his old university at Fenner's, taking 5 for 45 and 7 for 43. Nor were his triumphs restricted to the first-class game.

In the Benson and Hedges Cup match against Hampshire at Hove, 30 May and 1 June, he took 5 for 35 as the visitors were dismissed for 194. Sussex

Ian Greig returns to the dressing-room after the completion of another satisfactory innings.

tottered a little in reply, but he played a responsible innings of 51, and his side went on to win by three wickets with one ball to spare. He took the Gold Award.

Six weeks later, in the NatWest Bank Trophy match against Warwickshire at Edgbaston, he had another inspired day with an innings of 82 and 4 for 31, including the final spell of 3 for 6 in 2.5 overs to end the match, performances which brought him the man-of-the-match award.

Ian Greig had enjoyed a memorable and exciting season. Sussex cricket seemed on the brink of the best period in their history. The foundations had been built by Tony Greig, and now, with John Barclay an intelligent leader, it seemed that the all-round abilities of Ian Greig, Imran Khan and Barclay himself, the bowling of Arnold, Waller and le Roux, and the batting of Mendis, Parker, Gould and Colin Wells must bring honours to the club. The 1982 season was anticipated with eagerness, yet there were some disquieting dissensions in the committee room.

One thing was assured. In Sussex and England, Ian Greig was Ian Greig, no longer 'Tony Greig's younger brother'. He had accomplished the first part of his mission.

If there was disappointment that Sussex slipped to eighth in the County Championship in 1982, there was delight that they took the John Player League for the first time. They were beaten only once, by Worcestershire at Horsham, and won the League by a margin of 12 points from Middlesex. Ian Greig made valuable all-round contributions throughout the season as he did in helping the side to the semi-final of the Benson and Hedges Cup.

If his batting did not have the consistency of the previous season, he still managed a century against Warwickshire at Edgbaston and was ever a threat when he was at the crease. His medium-pace bowling showed no sign of losing its potency and brought him 68 wickets in all matches. It was apparent that he was in the minds of the Test selectors who had been shattered by the defection of players of the calibre of Gooch, Boycott, Knott, Lever, Willey, Underwood and Larkins to the rebel tour of South Africa, when they named him in the MCC side for the opening game of the season against the Champion County, Nottinghamshire. Ian Greig did not figure in their calculations for the series against India, but a rather lacklustre performance in the final match of that series led them to look for some revitalizing talent for the First Test against Pakistan, who were also touring that summer. They turned to Ian Greig and Eddie Hemmings and recalled Mike Gatting, who had been scoring prolifically in county cricket.

The match was played at Edgbaston, and it would be wrong to suggest that the selection of Greig pleased everyone. The Press very often influence selections, but this had not been the case with Greig who had been chosen solely by Peter May and his co-selectors. There were sections of the Press who disagreed with their choice.

Ian Greig arrived in Birmingham on 28 July and was ushered to a dressing-room in which the England players were sitting. He recalls the warmth of the reception he received from Ian Botham, and the prank that was played on him.

'When I was shown into the room the first person to say anything was "Both", who shouted out, "Come on new boy. I've saved a seat for you next to me". Peter May was talking, and I was handed a cup of tea. There was a television screen in one corner of the room. The picture was on, but the sound was turned off. "Both" suddenly turned to me and said, "There's your picture up there on the tele". I looked up, and when I did so he took his tea-spoon which he had left in his tea and pressed it on my hand. It was very hot and unexpected, and I dropped my cup of tea and

193

shouted out something very rude, which I certainly should not have said to the chairman of selectors who was trying to address us. Everybody roared with laughter, especially "Both" who slapped me on the back and said, "You'll do, boy. You'll be all right".

'That evening, after dinner, I had a drink at the bar of the hotel and then said that I was off to bed. "No you're not", said "Both", "You are going to have a drink with me. If you go to bed now, you'll lie awake for hours worrying about tomorrow. You're going to have a drink and a chat and then go to bed." And he ordered large brandies all round.

'I had already been told that I was definitely playing, and Ian talked as we sipped the brandy and put me totally at my ease. He tried to give some idea of what it would be like, and then he told me to go to bed, and I slept peacefully.'

Bob Willis won the toss, and England batted so that Ian's direct involvement in the game was delayed a little. Imran Khan produced a splendid spell of fast bowling, and Abdul Qadir, although taking only one wicket, bemused all the batsmen, including Greig. Tavare, Gower and Miller were the only ones to cope adequately with the varied Pakistan attack. Imran took seven wickets, and England were out for 272. Ian Greig, batting at number eight, was in for 77 minutes, faced 55 balls, hit two fours and was finally out for 14. He showed determination and resilience, if seeming a little perplexed by the unaccustomed leg-spin of Abdul Qadir who was to bowl him for 7 in the second innings.

Ian Botham accounted for Mudassar before the close, and Ian Greig took his first Test wicket early next morning when he had night-watchman Tahir Naqqash caught behind by Bob Taylor. Bob Willis showed the newcomer the utmost consideration, bringing him into the attack early and asking him, to his surprise, what end he would like. Eventually, Pakistan were bowled out for 251.

In his report of the match, Christopher Martin-Jenkins wrote, 'Ian Greig bowled his medium-fast to a sensible line and length and though he was flattered a little by his figures, since three of his wickets were tail-enders, including the night-watchman Tahir, he nevertheless is a less ordinary bowler than he looks. With a good action, his control is better than that of his illustrious brother. He is less theatrical, steadier, less brilliant.

It was Greig who got Zaheer after that prolific player had made an ominously solid looking 40.

Ian Greig's figures were 4 for 53, which, by coincidence, were the same as Tony's figures in the second innings of his debut Test. He bowled only four overs in the second innings as England went on to win a fine match by 113 runs. There was no question that he would be in the party for the Second Test match at Lord's.

The game at Lord's proved to be one of the great events in Pakistan Test history. Mohsin Khan scored 200, and, on the last afternoon, he and Javed Miandad scored 77 in under an hour to take their side to a famous victory, their first at Lord's. England's troubles began before the match started when Greig arrived to find that Bob Willis was unable to play because of a stiff neck and that Geoff Miller had gone down with chicken-pox. Jackman came in for Willis, but there was a dreadful sameness about the England attack — Jackman, Botham, Pringle, Greig and the spinner Hemmings. Botham was really the only one above medium-pace at that time.

Ian Greig says that the instructions that were given were that they should primarily adopt a defensive attitude and that the bowlers should maintain a line of attack outside the off stump. That was not something that he was accustomed to do, but although he found it difficult, he was the most economic of the England bowlers, his 13 overs costing 42 runs whilst Pakistan reached 428 for 8 declared. Bewildered by Abdul Qadir on the Saturday, England followed on and were bemused by the gentle swing of Mudassar Nazar on the Sunday. Greig made 3 and 2, and it was to be another seven years before he again became part of Test selectors' calculations, and then in very different circumstances.

He had bowled commendably, fielded well and had been as foxed as anybody, Lamb and Botham included, by the leg spin of Abdul Qadir. He was more a victim of the selection which had given England an unbalanced attack, with four medium-pace bowlers, one of whom, inevitably, had to be surplus to requirements.

There was no reason to believe at this stage that Ian Greig would pass out of contention for a Test place. He was one of the most exciting of all-rounders, capable of turning the course of a game with either bat or ball. Nor was there any reason to suggest that he had yet reached his peak.

In 1979, he had toured Japan and Australia with the Cambridge University rugby side, and, while in Brisbane, he had been approached by the University of Queensland, who had asked him to return the following year, 1980-81, to coach their cricket team. It was an offer he was happy to accept. In his first season in Brisbane, finding himself in need of haircut, he was directed to a salon by a friend. The salon was owned and run by a beautiful young lady named Cheryl Day. As Ian says, stroking his thinning locks, 'She didn't do too much for my hair'. He did find her very attractive, however, and asked her out. Their relationship grew and on 8 January 1983, they were married.

Ian returned to England for the start of the 1983 season, bristling with confidence and determined to regain his place in the Test side. He could not have wished for a better start. Sussex's opening match was against Oxford University in The Parks. Put in to bat,

January 1983 and Ian marries Cheryl Day.

they were struggling on 69 for 4 at lunch and were also missing Colin Wells, who had suddenly been taken ill. Ian Greig went in and played a dashing innings. He and Pigott, 27, aded 101 for the eighth wicket, and Ian finished on 147 not out. He had hit two sixes and fourteen fours in the third, and highest, century of his career.

Torrential rain over the weekend caused the match to be abandoned, and that was the pattern for much of May. He hit 59 in the victory over Somerset at Taunton and took 4 for 42 in the Whitsuntide match at Lord's.

Cheryl had remained in Brisbane in order to wind up her business affairs which included selling the salon. She arrived in Brighton in the first week in June. Tony and his wife were also in England, for Tony was part of the commentary team for the Prudential World Cup. On Saturday, 8 June, Sussex began their Championship match against Kent at Hove, and the four Greigs and Derek Underwood and Alan Knott dined together in the evening.

Sussex had batted in a rather pedestrian manner and there had been little sparkle in the game until Ian Greig, batting at number seven, had hit a brisk 42 in a stand of 73. After a good meal, the two Kent players returned to their hotel, and the Greigs returned to Ian's flat. He turned the key in the lock of the door, and the key snapped. A window had been left half-open, so it was felt that the only way into the flat was for Ian to climb through the window and open the door from the inside. He pulled himself on to the window ledge and stood to open the window wider. The ledge gave way and Ian fell and broke his ankle.

Cheryl was to spend the first fortnight of her time in England driving her husband from hospital to hospital for treatment. Sussex offered to pay him for the rest of the season and to allow him to return to Australia, but he refused and was adamant that he

Another boundary? Ian Greig punches the ball away.

would be fit enough to play again in August. He was right. The determination that had seen him through so much else was to see him back in the Sussex side for the John Player League game at Eastbourne on 7 August. He took two Derbyshire wickets for 28 runs. His two wickets came from successive deliveries when the visitors seemed to be cruising to victory, and eventually Sussex won by two runs. By the end of the month, he was fit enough to resume his place in the Championship side.

He concentrated on regaining full fitness in time for the start of the 1984 season, and once again he started well with 106 not out against Cambridge University in the second match of the season. He and Paul Parker shared an unbroken sixth-wicket partnership of 177. Greig hit 14 fours and batted for 133 minutes. He always loved to hit the ball.

It was a satisfactory season, with 813 runs, 62 wickets and 17 catches, the majority taken at slip. In spite of the fact that Imran Khan was out for the whole season and Pigott played only a few games, Sussex climbed to sixth in the Championship and finished third in the John Player Sunday League where Ian Greig batted with great flair and consistency and bowled economically. He was a tremendous favourite with the Sussex fans, epitomizing, as he did, the joyous and enthusiastic approach which is really at the heart of cricket on the south coast.

Behind the scenes, all was not well at Hove, and it was no secret that there was a certain amount of tension between the coach, Stewart Storey, and some of the players. The tactful captaincy of John Barclay did much to ease the tension. 'He was very special,' says Ian, 'He was in the Brearley mould. He understood his players and knew how to motivate them. He treated each one as an individual and realized that each one had to be handled in a particular way.'

In December 1984, Cheryl gave birth to their first

Tony, Ian and Michelle.

child, Michelle, so that they returned to England five months later, happy and confident as a family, little suspecting that they were about to face one of the most troubled periods of their lives.

In the Press, Sussex were freely tipped to be one of the leading sides of the season, but this note of optimism was not long sustained. They were to make a spirited effort over the final stages of the Sunday League and to finish second to Essex by a margin of two points. By then, however, the season had turned sour.

Gehan Mendis was very close to scoring five centuries in six successive first-class innings. He completed his fourth century in the first innings of the match against Hampshire at Portsmouth and was 96 not out in the second innings when Barclay declared. He had received only four balls in the preceding five overs, and he was far from pleased. Barclay defended his action as being tactical. He needed to declare and set Hampshire a target of 327 in 83 overs. Most felt that he had been ungenerous to his opening batsman. The match was drawn.

A few days later it was announced that Ian Greig would not be retained at the end of the season as the Sussex club had to make economies and could not afford his wages. The news took everyone in the cricket world by surprise. In *The Cricketer,* Alan Lee wrote: 'Sussex players were devastated by their committee's oddly-timed decision to sack popular all-rounder Ian Greig.

'Although the order to release a capped player came from the county's Finance Committee, whose concern over next year's budget is well founded, Greig's teammates are shocked at the way in which a recent England player was banished.

'Some feel that it would have been possible to gain local sponsorship to keep Greig at Hove where, since 1980, he has scored 4,000 runs and taken almost 300 wickets.

'Greig — younger brother of the former Sussex and England captain Tony — was troubled by a serious knee injury two years ago but felt that he had totally recovered his fitness this season and he had no immediate thought of retiring at the age of 29.

'He had not been in good form this year but remains an able and talented cricketer, especially in the one-day competitions. Several counties have already expressed interest in securing his registration but Greig is keeping his options open and if disenchantment sets in after such a blow, he is likely to end up pursuing a business career in Sydney, where brother Tony is chief of an insurance company.'

The Greigs were shattered by the news, and to this day, the only official reason for Sussex's action was the one that was given, the needs of economy. That the club was struggling at the time is undeniable. An ageing committee was finding it difficult to come to terms with modern needs of management and commerce, and rumour of dissension had been rife for some years. Greig was exceedingly popular among his fellow players and with the followers of the county, so that it must have been anticipated that his dismissal would cause much adverse comment. There were those who believed that the relationships between Stewart Storey and the players had much to do with Greig's departure and with that of Gehan Mendis, who went to Lancashire at the end of the season. A fine side was broken up far too quickly.

One theory is that Stewart Storey believed that Greig was the leader of the group of players who were opposed to him and manipulated his dismissal. Certainly, Storey and Greig had their differences, but Greig has always confronted men openly when he has disagreements with them. He is a man incapable of duplicity, and Storey was very much mistaken if he believed him to be the leader of some underground faction.

The departure of Greig solved none of Sussex's problems. Storey was blamed for much of the bad feeling in the dressing-room, and within a year of Ian's dismissal he was sacked, even though the county had no immediate replacement.

None of this was to help to the Greigs. The bottom had dropped out of Ian's world. There were enquiries from several counties and talks with Worcestershire, Glamorgan and Somerset. It seemed most likely that he would join the cider county where his old colleague Peter Roebuck was very keen to have him, but another old friend had just announced his retirement from cricket. Nigel Popplewell, having hit a double century against Essex at Southend, had said that he was no longer enjoying his cricket with Somerset and would leave at the end of the season. That county was in the midst of the great revolution which saw the end of their Botham, Richards, Garner era, and Ian had had enough of cricket politics for a while.

He returned to Brisbane, coaching and captaining Brisbane Colts and running a sports centre. It seemed that first-class cricket had lost one of its most joyful players.

Resurrection

I AN Greig did not give up hope of returning to first-class cricket. There was still a possibility of playing for Somerset in 1986, but telephone conversations with Peter Roebuck in Sydney in March of that year convinced him that it was not the course to take at the time, and so he settled in Brisbane.

An offer came from Barry Maranta, a business partner of Greg Chappell's, to follow a career in the business world, but he declined it although he considered the offer both kind and generous. The truth was that he was low in confidence. He ran the indoor school, he coached cricket, and if his qualifications could have been better, he had a general sense of financial security. More than anything, he felt that he was ambling through life, and for a man who had driven himself to attain targets, who was full of vitality and commitment and who had wanted nothing more than to succeed as a professional cricketer, this was a less than satisfactory existence. No cricketer finds it easy when his career comes to an end; when that end comes prematurely, unexpectedly and with a touch of cruelty, it is doubly difficult to endure.

On 20 January 1987, Cheryl gave birth to the Greigs' second child, Andrew. She brought the baby home from hospital five days later, and the same day Ian Greig received a telephone call from England. The caller was Geoff Arnold, Ian's former teammate in the good days at Sussex and now coach of Surrey, with whom he had spent the better part of his career. Arnold told Greig that, with Monkhouse having retired and Butcher having been released, Surrey felt they needed an experienced all-rounder and that they would like to offer him terms.

Ian and Cheryl with Michelle and Andrew.

Ian was both delighted and surprised. The call was totally unexpected. He said that he was certainly most interested in the offer, but he would like time to think it over and to discuss the terms. It was agreed that he should be allowed time to reach a decision, but before he had finally made up his mind he received another call from Arnold. Surrey were offering him the captaincy.

Surrey had three captains in four years and although there had been, and was, much talent in the side, there were players who were performing below their capabilities. It was also general knowledge that the dressing-room was not harmonious, and that the club had its problems in this area. To be captain of Surrey would be no sinecure.

It was the sort of challenge that Ian Greig relished, but he needed reasurrance that he was doing the right thing. He went to Sydney and spoke to Mickey Stewart, who was still part of the Surrey establishment, and he contacted his brother Tony and asked his advice.

Tony told Ian to consider three points, and his reaction to them would tell them both whether or not he should accept the captaincy. First, he said that if Ian was interested in taking the job because the financial offer was such a good one, then he should not take it. Second, he said that if he wanted to be captain of Surrey so that he could, in some way, get his own back at Sussex for the way in which they had treated him, then he should not be captain. 'If, however,' said Tony, 'you want to captain Surrey because you want to get back to the game you love and you think that you can do a good job, then say yes straight away and start packing.'

Ian knew that the reasons he wanted to captain Surrey were encapsulated in what Tony had said. Stewart had told him that Surrey felt that he was the sort of man who could unravel their problems, but there were still affairs to be determined before the appointment could be finalized.

There were concerns over his fitness, especially regarding the knee which had troubled him, and he was asked to see the Australian Board's medical officer in Brisbane. The report to Surrey indicated that Greig was a highly-motivated sportsman with a leg that was not good, but he had the dedication and resolve and general physical fitness that would surmount any problems. A further medical examination and interview in London later confirmed the Australian report that they believed he would overcome any difficulties.

As chairman of Surrey, Derek Newton was justified in saying that he could not recommend to his General Committee the appointment of Greig as captain of the county until he had met him and spoken to him himself. Accordingly, Ian was asked to fly to England and was booked into the hotel at Gatwick Airport for two days under the name of Ian Heseltine.

In a sport that is noted for its leaks of information on Test teams and other would-be 'secret' matters, it is astonishing how the news of Surrey's approach to Ian Greig was kept from the Press, but nothing was reported in the media until the appointment was officially announced. At Gatwick, Ian met Raman Subba Row, Derek Newton, Jimmy Fulford and Mickey Syewart, the chairman of the Cricket Committee. Surrey knew what they wanted, and they were quickly reassured that they were right in their choice of Greig. He had the belief in traditional values, the sense of discipline, the determination and the exuberance that they needed, and the appointment was confirmed.

He prepared for the job thoroughly. On the domestic front, Cheryl insisted that they should not become a family commuting from Australia. They would settle in England for at least as long as Ian remained with Surrey, and, with the guidance and help of the club, they bought a house in Woking. Professionally, Ian talked tactics with Tony for hours on end, and he spoke, too, to John Barclay for whom his admiration has never dwindled. He remembered and stored incidents in his career, like his debut for England when Bob Willis had said to him, 'Which end do you want? This is no different to county cricket. Do the same as you do at Sussex.'

The news of Greig's appointment had been kept within the confines of the Surrey committee room until March, and when it was released it was greeted with astonishment. In the April issue of *The Cricketer*, Alan Lee was quick to see the irony of a situation which had Greig arriving at The Oval and Storey leaving Hove at one and the same time. He pointed out that Storey had been a member of a Surrey side known

Ian Greig, a surprise but inspired choice as Surrey's new skipper.

'for solid on-field performances but rather more for bitchiness in the dressing room'. His relationships with players at Sussex had been strained, and after the dismissal of Greig, 'mightily popular, not to mention influential', there was open criticism of Storey, who had allegedly made little effort to keep Greig. 'For a time, it seemed there might be open revolt. Then, however, Greig himself did something to calm the situation.'

The Sussex troubles erupted again early in 1987, when Colin Wells became the second good class player to threaten to walk out of the county. Eight others followed in his wake and the outcome was that the players received an increase of approximately £2,000 a year each and Storey was sacked. As he left Sussex, Greig arrived at Surrey. The wheel had turned full circle in a year.

It was common knowledge that Surrey were seeking a captain from outside their staff to replace Pat Pocock. Jack Richards and Trevor Jesty had both stated their interest in the job, but, for reasons which were to become apparent in the coming months, both were considered to be unsuitable. Whatever the surprise at the appointment of Greig, there were those who discerned it could prove to be inspirational. As Lee concluded, 'Greig is abrasive and committed, yet his ambitions have never blinded him to the more sensitive demands of a team game. I suspect he will relish the challenge at The Oval, where he may well have a barrier or two to break down before peace reigns in the dressing-room.' These proved to be prophetic words.

Ian Greig is a man of transparent honesty. It is a quality which tends to humble those with whom he comes in contact. He knew what awaited him at The Oval. He knew that the dressing-room atmosphere had been bad, that there was much back-biting and an undercurrent of petty jealousies. To cure this state of affairs was his first priority. Just as he had disregarded

Ian had a good start to his Surrey career, 46 and 50 not out against Notts.

the information that former Surrey players were eager
to give him about the committee men, so he chose
to make his own judgements on the playing staff. For
him, everyone started with a clean sheet. All disagreements, all complaints and grievances would, from now
on, be talked through in the open, face to face. Mistakes
and failures in matches would be discussed and
responsibilities apportioned and accepted. His passion
for the game and his own frankness made such a policy
acceptable. He never shirked a task that he asked of
others, and he was quickly tested.

All began well; Greig hit 46 and 50 not out in the

opening match against Nottinghamshire, and the top score of 88 as Derbyshire were beaten by an innings at The Oval. All four Benson and Hedges matches were won in the zonal round and Surrey were rather unlucky to lose in the semi-final at Headingley, where they were maltreated by the weather. There were, inevitably, other days went things did not go so well, and, following one of them, the captain, as was his custom, went up to the committee room. There was something of a hush when he walked in, and the chairman came to him and said, 'I'm a bit surprised to see you here, captain. You've got some nerve, the way you batted, bowled and captained the side today.' Greig's reply was immediate. 'I think you and I should get one thing straight, chairman, if I can only come in here when we've had a good day, then you've got the wrong man.' It was language that Derek Newton understood and respected. From that day on, a special relationship has existed between the two men and no county captain could have had a more supportive chairman.

Ian Greig revealed what had been apparent to those who had seen him in his embryo days at Cambridge, that he had a rare gift of leadership. He was tough, fair, never afraid to make a decision, and he believed that a game does not deserve to be won unless one is also prepared to take a chance that may lose it.

There was a most remarkable example of this in the Sunday League game against Northamptonshire at Guildford. Surrey made 220 and, when the last over arrived, the visitors needed only four runs to win with six wickets remaining. Greig entrusted the last over to Monte Lynch, who had not bowled a ball in limited-over cricket all season and whose off-breaks were only occasionally brought into use. He had Harper caught behind, Williams stumped, and Cook was run out off the last ball to give Surrey victory by one run.

Whether he was successful or not when making a

Ian's gamble of handing the ball to Monte Lynch for the last over against Northants paid off handsomely.

The Surrey captain who won the respect of his players.

decision, Ian Greig was brave enough to stand by what he done. He was warm and encouraging, supportive of his players and won the respect of his team. The threat of disharmony began to disappear. Surrey, greatly aided by the two West Indian pace bowlers Gray and Clarke who, of course, could not play in the side together, finished fourth in the Championship.

There were hard decisions to be made at the end of the year and Greig faced these with the honesty that he had faced all else. One of the decisions was to release Trevor Jesty.

Jesty was a good club man. He had come from Hampshire where he had scored heavily, but been denied the captaincy which he believed he deserved. He had also wanted to be captain at The Oval, but he was thirty-nine years old, and pleasant as it was to have him in the side, if he remained at The Oval, it would mean limited opportunities for exciting young players like Jonathan Robinson, David Ward and Darren Bicknell. He was liked by all, but a choice had to be made, and Jesty, happily, found a new home in Lancashire.

Ian Greig's involvement with and commitment to Surrey did not end in the September. He was an integral and leading member of the administrative team that sought sponsorship and business throughout the winter in order to secure the financial future of the club, and of The Oval ground. His second season as captain was to present him with problems more taxing than those initially encountered.

Raman Subba Row had launched the *Save The Oval* appeal, and, with good business acumen and generous sponsorship, The Oval was saved. On and off the field, Ian Greig set about lifting the side to the professional standards that were essential if playing success was to be achieved and trophies were to be won. Of necessity, there was bloodshed.

Sylvester Clarke failed to arrive for a Sunday League

match at Swansea and was fined and suspended by the club. There were those who would have made the punishment more severe and more permanent, but Greig supported Clarke, believing that he still had a commitment to Surrey and something to give to its future.

In 1987, Clarke and Gray, playing in rotation, had captured 110 wickets between them in the Championship, but suspension and injury limited Clarke to 12 Championship matches in 1988, in which, nevertheless, he took 63 wickets. Tony Gray did not play in one Championship game.

He had sustained a broken arm in the Caribbean in the winter and had struggled for fitness. Inclusion in the West Indian team for the one-day series against Pakistan had suggested all was well again, but in England, he was able to find neither pace, energy, nor match-fitness, and he was not offered a contract for 1989. Nor, too, were David Smith and Jack Richards.

David Smith, a good left-handed batsman who played fast bowling well, had been with Surrey from 1973 to 1983 when he had not been re-engaged for personality and disciplinary reasons. He had played for Worcestershire for three seasons before returning to Surrey in 1987. A man on a short fuse, an easy prey to the pranks of others, something he was not always able to take in good part, Smith survived incidents of friction, with Greig's help, during the first year of his return to Surrey, but their recurrence in 1988 brought the inevitable result.

The dismissal of Jack Richards came as a surprise to many followers of Surrey who were not close to the game; to those in, and nearest to it, it came as no surprise at all. Richards could be a batsman of astonishing power and breadth of strokes. In his last season for Surrey, he played an amazing innings of 106 out of 139 in a winning Sunday League game against Essex. He was also a most capable wicketkeeper,

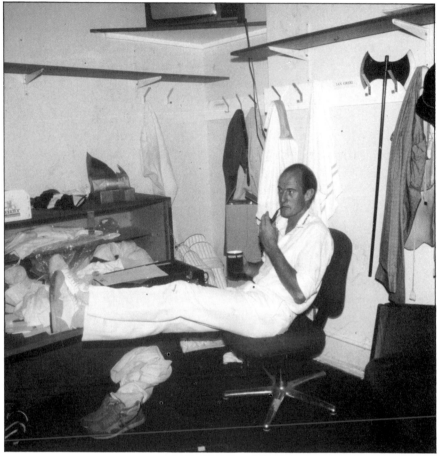

Difficult times in the Surrey dressing-room as the axe fell on Richards, Gray and Smith.

showing particular agility when keeping to the quicker bowlers. He toured India and Sri Lanka with Fletcher's side, 1981-82, as second wicketkeeper, and returned with a report on attitude that was less than flattering. He disappeared from the international scene, but he was later to win Test caps and score a century against Australia.

Richard's talent was undeniable, but so was the fact that he was highly-strung, and that his ambition warped his judgement to the extent that he was quoted

217

as saying that he found it difficult to play when he knew the captain was earning more than he was and that the Surrey appeal had destroyed his benefit. His contentiousness was a disturbing influence in the dressing-room, and if there was to be harmony in Surrey cricket, it was apparent that such harmony could only be achieved without Jack Richards. He seemed to draw little pleasure from the game and to feel that all were against him. It is significant that when he was released by Surrey, he was unable to find a place with another county.

If Richards, Smith, Clarke, Gray, and the financial difficulties brought about by the untrustworthiness of politicians were Surrey's, and Greig's problems in 1988, there was also much to be pleased about. There was fourth place in the County Championship and a semi-final place in the NatWest Bank Trophy. One felt that they had the beating of Middlesex, but they gave a below par performance on the day, and lost easily in spite of an Alec Stewart century. What was refreshing about the semi-final defeat was the honesty with which it was greeted. There were no excuses. There was an acceptance that they had played badly and had not deserved to win. They were young, and they were learning. Greig's influence was already biting deep.

There was high optimism for the 1989 season, but before any of the hopes could be realized there were disappointments. Under Ian Greig's recommendation, Surrey had signed Dirk Tazelaar, the left-arm pace bowler from Queensland, who was on the verge of the Australian side. Tazelaar was expected to ease the pressure on Sylvester Clarke, who had returned in March looking fit and well. By the beginning of the season, however, Clarke was overweight and it was obvious that he was not prepared to subject himself to the discipline and training needed to maintain standards at the top level. He was dismissed for 'persistent breaches of the terms and conditions of his contract'. For Enfield, in the Lancashire League, he made one appearance, bowling off-spinners off five paces. He was sacked immediately.

It was a sad end for one who had once been the most feared bowler in county cricket, and for Greig it was a bitter disappointment. 'He had bad knees, yes, but he could have been another Richard Hadlee if he had looked after himself and kept his weight down. He could bowl at the speed of lightning off his Sunday League run, and he could have done that for another three years.' Like all men of total dedication, Ian Greig has always been most saddened by those who waste god-given talents.

The loss of Clarke was not totally unexpected, but the failure of Tazelaar to come to expectations and then to break down with a back injury before the end of May most certainly was. Surrey faced 1989 without an overseas bowler and without Monte Lynch for the start of the season because of a broken leg sustained before the campaign began. Tony Murphy, acquired from Lancashire, was a tower of strength in the bowling, and, cajoled and encouraged by Greig, the exuberant young Surrey side moved towards maturity. If the results did not reflect their ability, their worth was recognized by the England selectors who, towards the end of the season, named five Surrey players in their two touring parties. Alec Stewart and Keith Medlycott were to be part of Gooch's side in a testing tour of the West Indies, whilst the Bicknell brothers and Graham Thorpe were included in the England 'A' side for Zimbabwe. There was a well-founded rumour that the England selectors came close to naming *six* Surrey players.

Although able to bowl little because of a troublesome knee injury, Ian Greig hit 1,013 first-class runs, average 42.20, another 438 runs in limited-over matches and led the side with decisiveness, zest and intelligence. He was generally regarded as the best captain in county

Top left: Andrew on his first day at school, pictured with his proud father. Ian's striped blazer was awarded to him by Surrey supporter Steve Kingshott, who makes a similar presentation to any Surrey batsman who scores a double century. Top right: A younger Andrew practising his driving with a tennis racket and golf ball. Bottom: Michelle looks on as her brother progresses to bat and ball.

cricket. England, led by David Gower, had been severely and unexpectedly mauled by Australia in the Test series and it was common knowledge that Gower would not be asked to lead the side to the Caribbean.

Some three or four days before the selectors met to decide on who was to captain England in the coming series against West Indies, Alan Lee in *The Times* revealed that Greig would be named as England captain. Lee, ever a journalist with an ear close to events, was confident in his statement, and his view was soon echoed by other notable cricket correspondents. These newspaper reports, followed by conversations with journalists, were the first intimation that Greig had that he was being considered, and the journalists were confident in their information that he would succeed Gower as England's captain.

He received telephone calls from the Test and County Cricket Board confirming his situation and his availability. He was then contacted by Lt-Col John Stephenson, acting in his capacity as secretary of the ICC rather than as secretary of MCC. John Stephenson said that he needed clarification on four points:

1. When Greig went to Australia at the end of the 1985 season in England, had he intended to stay there on a permanent basis?
2. Did he buy property in Australia?
3. Did he sell property in England?
4. Had he intended playing in England in 1986?

Ian Greig gave the simple and honest answers to all of these questions. He had gone to Australia with every intention of returning to England if he possibly could, that his wife was the only one who had ever owned property in Australia which was her native country, that they had sold no property in England because they had never had the finances to buy any in the first place, and that almost until the England season had started he had held out hopes of playing in England in 1986 and had gone to Sydney specifically to discuss the possibility with Peter Roebuck.

John Stephenson was totally satisfied with his response and told Ian that he would be in touch again shortly. He later phoned to say that unfortunately the ICC had put Ian's case to their lawyers who had advised that he was ineligible to play for England and that he required a further four-year residential qualification period. He remained recognized, however, as an English qualified player.

It is difficult for the expert, let alone the layman, to unravel the intricacies of a situation whereby a man who has been educated at an English university, who has played twice for England in Test matches, who has a father who is British and who, except for a period of eighteen months between 1985 and 1987, has lived in England since 1976, can be deemed as ineligible to play for England. Particularly as, during that period of eighteen months, he would, like the majority of professional cricketers, have been out of the country trying to earn a living. Ian Greig's frustration is that he will now never know whether, had the lawyers found in his favour, he would have been asked to take England to the West Indies in 1990, or even the England 'A' team to Zimbabwe.

As it was, he went to the Caribbean on another mission, to find Surrey a quick bowler. High on the shopping list was Ezra Moseley, re-establishing himself in domestic cricket in the West Indies and winning a place in the Test side against England after his years of banishment, but Moseley was not too keen on the rigours of first-class cricket in England and settled for the professional's job at Oldham in the Central Lancashire League. Greig and coach Geoff Arnold then turned their attention to Tony Gray, who was now fit and keen to return to Surrey. He had been highly recommended by John Holder and John Hampshire, who had seen him when they umpired in Zimbabwe

Ian Greig, the man who might have followed in his brother's footsteps and captained England.

and had nothing but praise for him. So Gray came back to The Oval to the surprise of many but also to their delight when they saw how enthusiastic he was. The enthusiasm waned a little when Gray began to experience fitness problems almost as soon as he arrived in April 1990, but before those problems became paramount, there was an extraordinary match at The Oval.

Surprisingly and disappointingly, Surrey lost their opening Championship match against Sussex at Hove. Gray broke down and could not bowl in the second

223

innings, nor was he available for the next match, against Lancashire at The Oval.

This was a four-day game, and Greig was happy to win the toss and bat first on a pitch which conformed to the TCCB's ideals of a batsman's paradise. Clinton went at 10, but Alikhan and Stewart added 108, and Monte Lynch made 95. Ian Greig came in at 275 for 5, and by the close, he and Medlycott had advanced the score to 396 for 6, and the captain had made 56. After the second new ball had been taken, the pair had added 61 in ten overs.

Before lunch on the second day, Ian Greig hit 145 runs, and the twelve overs after lunch produced 101 runs for Surrey. Of the 311 runs in fifty-five overs scored by Surrey on the second day, Greig made 235. He was caught on the long-on boundary in attempting to hit what would have been his tenth six, four of which had come in the space of five balls. He hit twenty-five fours, and his 291 came off only 251 balls in 277 minutes.

His innings was the highest by a Surrey batsman for 64 years, and he declared when Surrey had reached 707 for 9, the highest score ever made against Lancashire.

As has now passed into history, Lancashire replied with 863, of which Fairbrother scored 366, Atherton 191 and Mendis, highly rated by Greig, 102. One would not wish to detract in any way from Neil Fairbrother's magnificent achievement in beating the record that Len Hutton set up at The Oval in 1938, but after the last Test of the summer, against India at The Oval, Mike Atherton said that, with due respect to his county colleague and friend, he considered Ian Greig's innings to be the most astonishing and brilliant he has ever seen. Few who saw it would disagree with him. Rarely can there have been such sustained powerful striking of the ball over such a long period. Almost incidentally, his partnership of 205 with Martin Bicknell, 42,

'The most astonishing innings' – *Ian's 291 off 251 balls in 277 minutes.*

established a new Surrey record for the eighth wicket.

Greig himself believes that his innings of 123 not out against Somerset at Weston-super-Mare at the beginning of August was at least an innings of equal merit, for he had risen from a sick bed when his side was in deep trouble. He had been struck by a fever in the night and had slept hardly at all. He put on his pads and lay in a Portakabin alongside the dressing-room, hoping to sleep and asking to be called only when he was needed to bat. He had no time to close his eyes, for Surrey were very quickly 39 for 4.

With David Ward justifying the faith that his captain had shown in him and scoring more than 2,000 runs, Surrey's problem was again that of the overseas bowler. Gray was again out of action, and Ian Greig had to act quickly. In Dubai, he had met Imran Khan, who had spoken of Waqar Younis. He saw great potential in Waqar, but said, 'I don't think he's yet a number-one overseas player, but it would be good if you could offer him some second-team cricket to give him the opportunity to learn the game in England.'

When things were not going well with Tony Gray, Greig chased up Imran, who was in the United States. He asked what the position was regarding Waqar, and Imran replied that he had offered Waqar's services to Sussex in respect of what they had done for him. Sussex had said that they were not interested even though he was only asking for some second-team games for the lad. Imran had been very disappointed.

Greig's immediate response was that he would offer Waqar Younis a second-team game the following Wednesday, but that he should come to The Oval on the Tuesday to meet the rest of the team. He asked him to be there at ten o'clock, but Waqar arrived at nine. He was met by Greig, coach Geoff Arnold and Alec Stewart.

In Greig's eyes, Alec Stewart is the supreme professional. He will not take the field unless he is one hundred per cent fit, and he sets himself high standards of achievements. He put on the pads, and for forty minutes he batted in the nets while Waqar bowled. The three Surrey men had a brief conference and were agreed that they must sign him. Ian went to see secretary David Seward and said that Waqar Younis should be instantly registered as an 'A' category overseas player. Seward urged restraint, particularly as neither Subba Row nor the chairman was available and that the Surrey policy was for one overseas player only. Greig persuaded him and later Newton and Subba Row that the matter was urgent and essential, and Seward filed the registration immediately. Waqar played at Old Trafford in the Benson and Hedges Cup the next day. He did not bowl well, but within weeks the other sixteen counties knew that Surrey had struck gold.

Raman Subba Row queried the contract given to Waqar, for it was club policy to have only one overseas player under contract, since that was soon to be the TCCB ruling, but the trust between those in authority at The Oval is such that Subba Row was quick to appreciate that there had been a need for immediate action. Gray was bitterly disappointed, but for the second time in three years, he had failed to maintain fitness, and he was released.

Overall, the playing results in 1990 were disappointing although Medlycott was the first to fifty wickets and was one of the five Surrey players who were again selected for England tours. Greig enjoyed the best batting season of his career, 1,259 runs, average 54.73, an outstanding performance for one often at number seven.

There was, perhaps, frustration among some of the young players, impatient for success. In their immaturity, they often failed to see how hard their captain fought for them in the Committee Room as well as on the field. Ian Greig has never shirked any

Ian and Cheryl meet cricket fan John Major.

problem, and he and Medlycott had a heart-to-heart talk for several hours when that player was losing faith in himself and others when form deserted him. The results were to be seen in the happy revival at the beginning of the 1991 season.

Greig is not afraid to confront his players when he thinks they have erred or are falling short of standards. He wants them to enjoy the game as much as he does, but he wants them also to know the time for fun and the time for work.

The Greigs are inextricably entangled with cricket. When the MCC sent a side to Namibia at the beginning of 1991, it was managed by Phil Hodson, Sally Greig's husband; and the Namibian side was managed by N.O.Curry, Molly's husband.

Ian Greig has made no promises to Surrey, and he has asked only one thing, that when they win the Championship, as he believes they will with the exciting young talent that has emerged and which he has helped to foster, it may not be in his time, but he asks that Surrey fly him from wherever he is to join in the celebrations. It is the least he deserves.

He is now in charge of cricket at The Oval. 'The buck stops' with Ian Greig. There is a trusting, vulnerable innocence about him which makes one believe that he could be so easily cheated and betrayed by those whom he has befriended and aided, but he would not want one to show concern over such a belief. He has an honesty and integrity which gives him sufficient strength in himself. He has long since emerged from the shadow of his brother and become his own man. He is no longer two paces behind Tony.

He has followed his father's precept, 'to thine own self be true', and he has been false to no man. He has made a mark on the history of cricket which, if softer than that made by his brother and less controversial, is just as indelible.

Ian and Tony pictured at the Foster's Oval in May 1990.

Statistics

Tony Greig

Batting

Matches 350; innings 579; not outs 45; runs 16,660; highest score 226; average 31.19; centuries 26.
Catches 345.

Test Matches

Matches 58; innings 93; not outs 4; runs 3,599; highest score 148; average 40.43; centuries 8; fifties 20.
Catches 87.

Bowling

856 wickets for 24,702 runs, average 28.85.
Five wickets in an innings 33.
Ten wickets in a match 8.

Test Matches

141 wickets for 4,541 runs, average 32.50.
Five wickets in an innings 6.
Ten wickets in a match 2.

Ian Greig

(complete until 30 September, 1990)

Batting

Matches 233; innings 308; not outs 46; runs 7,691; highest score 291; average 29.35; centuries 8. Catches 145.

Test Matches

Matches 2; innings 4; not outs 0; runs 26; highest score 14; average 6.50.

Bowling

409 wickets for 12,597 runs, average 30.79. Five wickets in an innings 10. Ten wickets in a match 2.

Test Matches

4 wickets for 114 runs, average 28.50. Best 4 for 53.

Select Bibliography

The Art of Captaincy J.M.Brearley
The Return of the Ashes J.M.Brearley & Dudley Doust
I Declare Mike Denness
The Family Fortune Alan Hill
Captaincy Ray Illingworth
The All-Rounder Peter Walker
The Autobiography Geoff Boycott
The Players Ric Sissons
The Packer Affair Henry Blofeld
Wisden (various years)
Pelham Cricket Year,
Benson and Hedges Cricket Year,
The Cricketer
Bomber Squadron at War Andrew Brookes